The Art of Letting Go:

Stop Overthinking, Stop Negative Spirals, and Find Emotional Freedom

By Nick Trenton
nicktrenton.com

Table of Contents

Chapter 1: The Art of Letting Go

Letting go can be one of the most challenging and yet transformative experiences in life. Whether it's letting go of a relationship, a job, a dream, a belief, or a behavior, the act of releasing something that individuals have held on to for a long time can feel like a loss, a failure, or a betrayal of themselves. At the same time, however, it can also be liberating, empowering, and enlightening as individuals open themselves up to new possibilities, insights, and growth.

This is a powerful book that offers readers a new perspective on the art of releasing emotional burdens. Whether individuals are struggling to let go of a past relationship or trying to break free from negative thought patterns, this book is a must-read. Written with deep compassion and insight, it empowers readers to shed the weight of emotional baggage and find the courage to move on to a happier, healthier future. Drawing upon both life experiences and psychological techniques, the author reveals the secrets to releasing what no longer serves humans and embracing the beauty of letting go.

The book delves into topics such as self-awareness, acceptance, forgiveness, gratitude, mindfulness, compassion, and resilience, and shows how they can foster a sense of inner peace, clarity, and purpose. The book also addresses common myths and misconceptions about letting go, such as the idea that it means giving up or forgetting, and offers a more nuanced and empowering perspective that honors our past, present, and future selves.

Whether individuals are struggling with a particular challenge or seeking to cultivate a more mindful and meaningful life, this book will provide them with insights and inspiration to help them let go of what no longer serves them and embrace what does.

Is everyone ready to embark on this journey of letting go?

Letting go is often used in psychology to describe the process of releasing attachment to something or someone. It may refer to letting go of negative thoughts, emotions, or behaviors that hold an individual back from reaching their full potential. At its core, letting go is all about surrendering control and allowing oneself to move on from situations that may no longer serve a person's best interests.

As the reader begins this chapter, they will be introduced to three important concepts: dichotomy of control, nonjudgmental thinking, and self-distancing. Each of these ideas builds on one another, offering a key understanding of how to approach various situations in life. On one hand, the principle of dichotomy of control emphasizes the importance of focusing on what can be controlled, rather than worrying about the things that cannot. This concept is especially useful when trying to navigate certain challenges or obstacles.

Meanwhile, nonjudgmental thinking encourages the reader to approach situations with an open and accepting mind free from biases and assumptions. Finally, the concept of self-distancing offers techniques for gaining a more objective perspective, particularly when dealing with emotionally charged situations. These three concepts work in tandem to help the reader cultivate a more balanced and effective approach to problem-solving and decision-making.

DICHOTOMY OF CONTROL

"Some things are within our power, while others are not. Within our power are opinion, motivation, desire, aversion, and, in a word, whatever is of our own doing; not within our power are our body, our property, reputation, office, and, in a word, whatever is not of our own doing." —Epictetus

The dichotomy of control is a central concept in Stoic philosophy that emphasizes the importance of distinguishing between things that are within one's control and things that are beyond one's control. According to this doctrine, people should focus their efforts on the things that are under their control and accept the things that are not.

To illustrate this concept, consider a student who is preparing for an exam. The student has control over certain things, such as their study habits, their level of focus, and their time management. However, they do not have control over the difficulty level of the exam, the questions that will be asked, or the grading criteria.

By focusing on the things that are within their control, the student can develop a study plan, manage their time effectively, and maintain their focus. However, if they spend too much time worrying about the things that are beyond their control, such as the exam's difficulty level, they may become anxious and stressed, which can negatively affect their performance.

Another example of the dichotomy of control can be seen in relationships. In a romantic relationship, one partner cannot control the other's thoughts or feelings. However, they can control their own actions and reactions in response to their partner. By focusing on their own behavior and communication, they can contribute to a healthy relationship. Conversely, if they spend too much energy trying to change their partner's behavior or worrying about things they cannot control, it may create conflict and damage the relationship.

Consider John. He is a man of extreme order and control. He has always been that way, even as a child. Every detail in his life has to be perfect, from the way he keeps his house to the way he runs his business and his relationships. It all just seems so natural for him; controlling everything around him is like second nature.

But then one day, something changes. John meets someone who challenges his perception of control and freedom—a woman named Olivia. She is wild and carefree, living by her own rules rather than following anyone else's orders or schedules. Somehow she just gets under John's skin in an irresistible way; it feels like she can see right through him and knows exactly how to push all the right buttons to make him question things about himself he'd never thought twice about before meeting her.

The more they hang out together, the more their differences begin to blur until eventually they find themselves at an impasse: either John accepts Olivia's brand of chaos into his tightly controlled world, or he risks losing her altogether if he tries too hard to keep her within its boundaries. There doesn't seem any other option available anymore but this dichotomy between having total control over everything or giving up some of that power for true happiness with another person as well as himself. In the end, after much soul-searching (and maybe a few arguments too), John comes out on top with a newfound understanding that sometimes letting go can be just what one needs in order for their life, and those around them, to thrive! John knows that holding too tightly on to the past and ruminating over what-ifs will only serve to hold him back in life.

Therefore, he consciously decides to let go of the things he has no control over (major life events, circumstances, feelings, individuality) and chooses to focus on things he can control, such as being present, accepting, empathetic, and loyal. The dichotomy of control helps him focus his efforts on the things that truly matter and accept the things that are beyond his control. It encourages him to take responsibility for his actions and reactions, rather than blaming external circumstances or other people for his problems.

Epictetus was a prominent Stoic philosopher who emphasized the importance of living in accordance with reason, virtue, and the natural order of the universe. In his teachings, he often stressed the importance of focusing on what is within one's control and letting go of what is outside of it. This advice may seem paradoxical at first, but it reflects the Stoic view of the world and an individual's place in it.

According to Stoic philosophy, the universe is governed by a rational and benevolent force called the logos, which is responsible for creating and maintaining the order and harmony of the cosmos. The logos ensures that everything happens for a reason and that there is a purpose behind all events, even if people don't always understand it. This belief in divine providence and the rationality of the universe is what allows the Stoics to be confident about things they can't control.

At the same time, the Stoics recognize that there are things people *can* control, such as their thoughts, emotions, and actions. It is in these areas that people should focus their attention and efforts. By cultivating the right mindset and living in accordance with reason and virtue, people can achieve inner peace, freedom, and a good life, regardless of external circumstances.

One of the most important gifts that nature has given humans, according to the Stoics, is the ability to reason. Unlike animals, people have the power to reflect on their thoughts, emotions, and actions, and to choose how they want to live their lives. This ability to reason is what makes them human and gives them the potential for greatness. Epictetus' advice to be confident about things people can't change and careful about things they can change reflects the Stoic worldview and their emphasis on living in accordance with reason, virtue, and the natural order of the universe. By focusing on what is within one's control and cultivating the right mindset, people can achieve inner peace, freedom, and a good life, regardless of external circumstances.

Epictetus believed in the importance of using the three faculties of the mind wisely. Specifically, he outlined the "dichotomy of control," which highlights these faculties as essential to one's well-being. The faculty of judgment governs the way people think, feel, and believe. The faculty of desire guides one's desires and fears. The faculty of will directs one's intentions, decisions, and actions. Using these faculties in proper balance can allow people to live a fulfilling and virtuous life. Epictetus' teachings are a reminder that people have the power to shape their own experiences and must take responsibility for their thoughts and actions in order to live a happy and meaningful life.

The wise use of these faculties, he argued, was the key to living a good life.

The faculty of judgment is responsible for one's thoughts, emotions, and beliefs. It allows people to make judgments about what is true and false, good and bad, and right and wrong. Epictetus believed that people should use this faculty to develop accurate and rational beliefs about the world. They should strive to avoid making judgments based on emotions, biases, or prejudices. For example, imagine that a person receives criticism from their boss. Their initial emotional response might be to feel angry or defensive. However, using their faculty of judgemnt, they can reflect on the situation and try to understand the criticism objectively. This can help them make a rational decision about how to respond.

The faculty of desire is responsible for one's desires and fears. It allows them to seek pleasure and avoid pain. Epictetus believed that people should use this faculty to develop rational desires and to avoid irrational fears. We should strive to desire only those things within one's control and to avoid fearing things that are not. For example, imagine that an individual desires a promotion at work. This is a rational desire, as it is something within their control. However, if they fear losing their job, this is an irrational fear, as it is not within their control. By using their faculty of desire wisely, they can focus on achieving their goals without being held back by irrational fears.

The faculty of will is responsible for one's intentions, decisions, and actions. It allows people to act on their desires and to make decisions about how to live their lives. Epictetus believed that people should use this faculty to make wise decisions and to take responsible actions. People should strive to act in accordance with their rational desires and to avoid acting impulsively or irresponsibly. For example, imagine that someone has a desire to become more physically fit. Using their faculty of will, they can decide to join a gym and create a workout plan. They can then take action by following through on their plan and making regular visits to the gym. By using their faculty of will wisely, they can achieve their goals and live a healthier life. The wise use of the three faculties of the mind is the key to living a good life. By using one's faculty of judgment to develop rational beliefs, one's faculty of desire to seek rational desires, and one's faculty of will to make responsible decisions and take action, individuals can achieve their goals and live a fulfilling life.

How to Practice and Apply the Dichotomy of Control

The dichotomy of control may sound like a complicated concept, but it's actually a simple technique that can have a powerful impact on one's life. At its core, it's a philosophy that encourages people to focus only on those things they can control, and to let go of everything else. This might seem counterintuitive at first, but it's a mindset that can help them navigate life's ups and downs with greater ease and resilience. Of course, like any skill, putting the dichotomy of control into practice takes practice, but with time and effort, it can become second nature. Whether one is facing a difficult work situation, a challenging relationship, or just the everyday stresses of life, embracing the dichotomy of control can help them maintain a sense of inner calm and clarity.

Step 1 involves developing a constant focus on the present moment. A crucial aspect of the Stoic practice of the dichotomy of control is cultivating a constant focus on the present moment. This means training one's mind to be fully engaged with what is happening right now, rather than being distracted by worries or regrets about the past, or anxieties or expectations about the future.

One way to develop this sort of focus is through mindfulness meditation. Mindfulness is the practice of paying attention to the present moment with an attitude of curiosity, openness, and nonjudgment. By regularly practicing mindfulness, people can train their minds to become more aware of their thoughts, emotions, and sensations, and to stay grounded in the present moment. Here's an example of how to apply mindfulness in everyday life, using the example of a morning routine:

Waking up in the morning, individuals are advised to take a few deep breaths and bring attention to their body and their surroundings. As they get out of bed, they notice the sensation of their feet touching the floor, the temperature of the room, and the sounds around them. As they brush their teeth, they need to pay attention to the sensation of the bristles against their teeth and gums, the taste of the toothpaste, and the movements of their hands and arms. As they take a shower, they feel the water on their skin, smell the soap or shampoo, and notice any thoughts or feelings that arise. Throughout the morning routine, they try to stay present and engaged with each moment, rather than letting one's mind wander or getting lost in thoughts or worries about the day ahead. By cultivating this sort of present-moment awareness, people can begin to develop a deeper sense of inner peace and calm and become better equipped to navigate the ups and downs of daily life.

One other example of a mindfulness technique to stay in the present moment is body scan meditation. In this technique, a person lies down or sits comfortably and focuses their attention on each part of their body, starting from their toes and moving up toward their head. As they focus on each body part, they become aware of any sensations or feelings they may be experiencing in that area, without judgment or analysis. This helps them become more present in the moment and to cultivate a sense of relaxation and awareness in their body. Here's how to incorporate this into one's routine:

Find a quiet and comfortable place where you can lie down or sit without distractions. You can use a yoga mat, a cushion, or a chair for support. Close your eyes and take a few deep breaths, letting go of any tension in your body. Start by focusing your attention on your toes. Pay attention to any sensations you may be feeling in your toes, such as warmth, tingling, or tension. Don't judge or analyze the sensations—simply observe them.

Slowly move your attention to the rest of your feet, noticing any sensations or feelings. Continue to move your attention up your legs, to your thighs, hips, lower back, abdomen, chest, arms, hands, neck, and finally your head. Spend a few moments on each body part, being aware of any sensations or feelings that arise. If you notice any tension or discomfort, simply acknowledge it and let it go, without trying to change or fix it. If your mind starts to wander, gently bring your attention back to the present moment and continue with the body scan.

When you reach the top of your head, take a few deep breaths and allow yourself to rest in this state of relaxation and awareness. When you're ready, slowly open your eyes and take a few more deep breaths before getting up.

People can do a body scan meditation for as little as five minutes or as long as thirty minutes, depending on their schedule and preferences. It can be a helpful way to reduce stress, improve sleep quality, and cultivate mindfulness in their daily life.

Step 2 of practicing the dichotomy of control is to develop the habit of constantly asking oneself whether a given situation or circumstance is under their control. This involves being mindful of one's thoughts and reactions and questioning whether they have any power to change the situation at hand.

For example, imagine a person is driving to work and gets stuck in traffic. They may feel frustrated and anxious about being late, but by applying the dichotomy of control, they would ask themselves, "Is the traffic under my control?" The answer is no, as they cannot control the flow of traffic. Therefore, they would remind themselves that the traffic is none of their concern and that they should focus on what they can control, such as their reactions to the situation or how they use the time stuck in traffic, like listening to an audiobook or calling a friend.

Another example could be a student who receives a poor grade on an assignment. Instead of becoming upset and dwelling on the outcome, they can apply the dichotomy of control by asking themselves whether the grade is under their full control. The answer is no, as the grade has already been assigned and cannot be changed. Therefore, the student can choose to focus on what they can control, such as studying harder for the next assignment or seeking feedback from their teacher on how to improve.

Here's another example of how an individual can apply the habit of constantly asking oneself whether a given situation or circumstance is under their control: Tim is a manager at a software company, and he's working on a project that has been delayed due to technical difficulties. John is feeling frustrated and stressed about the situation because the delay is putting the project timeline at risk.

To apply the habit, Tim could pause and ask himself, "What aspects of this situation are under my control?" He might identify that he can communicate the delay to his team and stakeholders, prioritize critical tasks, and explore alternative solutions. Next, he could ask himself, "What aspects of this situation are not under my control?" He might recognize that he can't control the technical issues causing the delay or the fact that the project timeline is at risk.

By taking this step-by-step approach, Tim can better understand what actions he can take to address the situation and what actions he needs to let go of. He can then focus his energy on the things he can control, which can help him feel more empowered and productive. In this way, the habit of constantly asking oneself whether a given situation or circumstance is under their control can be a practical and actionable tool for managing stress and improving one's ability to navigate challenging situations.

Step 3 of practicing and applying the dichotomy of control seeks to answer the age-old question "*Is this under my control?*" If one's answer to this is "partially," Epictetus advises individuals to make the best of the situation and leave the rest to providence. This means that individuals should take responsibility for what they can control and influence to the best of their abilities, but also understand and accept that some aspects of a situation are beyond their control.

For example, imagine an individual is preparing for a job interview. They can control their preparation, attire, and attitude going into the interview. However, they cannot control the preferences and biases of the interviewer or the outcome of the interview. By recognizing this, the individual can focus on doing their best during the interview while also accepting that the ultimate decision is not in their hands.

In this way, the practice of leaving partial control to providence can help people avoid unnecessary stress and anxiety over situations they cannot control. By focusing on what they can control and accepting what they cannot, individuals can approach life with a sense of peace and equanimity, even in the face of challenges and adversity.

Life is unpredictable, and sometimes things just don't go according to plan. When faced with circumstances that might seem out of one's control, it's important to remember that not everything is entirely within one's grasp. However, that doesn't mean people should simply sit back and watch as life happens. Rather, they should strive to make the most of every situation, even if they can only control part of it. For instance, imagine an individual is planning an outdoor picnic with friends, but the weather doesn't look all that promising.

While they may not be able to control the weather, they can still bring some fun activities that don't require perfect weather, like board games or card games. Ultimately, by making the best out of what's partially under their control, they leave the rest up to fate and trust that things will turn out okay.

Here's another example of how an individual can apply the concept of partially controlling a situation and leaving the rest to providence: Samantha is a freelance writer who has been asked to submit a proposal for a high-profile project. She knows that this project could potentially lead to many more opportunities, and she is eager to impress the client. She spends a lot of time researching the project and putting together a strong proposal.

However, when Samantha submits her proposal, she finds out that there are several other highly qualified writers vying for the same project. At this point, Samantha realizes that the situation is only partially under her control. While she can control the quality of her proposal, she cannot control the decisions of the client or the actions of the other writers.

To make the best of the situation, Samantha focuses on the things she can control. She sends a follow-up email to the client, thanking them for the opportunity and offering to answer any additional questions they may have. She also spends time reaching out to other potential clients and working on other writing projects.

Samantha understands that there are factors outside of her control that could impact the outcome of the project. However, by focusing on what she can control, she feels more empowered and less anxious about the situation. She trusts that if this project is meant to be, it will be, and if not, there will be other opportunities in the future.

In this way, Samantha is able to apply the concept of partially controlling a situation and leaving the rest to providence, to her freelance writing career. By focusing on what she can control and accepting what she cannot, she is able to approach her work with greater resilience and a sense of peace, even in uncertain or challenging situations.

The Two-Minute Dichotomy of Control Meditation

Imagine a student struggling with their grades in a difficult course. They feel like they are doing everything they can to study and prepare, but they keep getting disappointing results on their exams.

To use the two-minute dichotomy of control meditation, the student will get a piece of paper and a pen. Then they draw a big circle on the paper and a smaller circle within it. In the smaller circle, they will write down the things that are within their control when it comes to their grades. For example, they could write something like:

- How much time they spent studying each day.
- How they studied (taking notes, reading the textbook, watching videos, etc.)

- Whether they asked questions in class or reached out to their professor for help.
- How they approached each exam (staying calm, reading each question carefully, double-checking their work, etc.)

In the larger circle, they could write down the things that were outside of their control. For example, they could write:

- How difficult the course material is.
- How the exams are structured and graded.
- How much time they have to complete each exam.
- Whether other students in the class are performing well.

These are all things they cannot control, no matter how hard they try. They may have contributed to their struggles, but there was nothing they could do to change them. Now that they have these two circles, they can begin to see where they can leverage what they have to improve their situation.

They can focus their energy and attention on the things within their control, such as studying more effectively or seeking help from their professor. They can let go of the things that are outside of their control, such as how difficult the course material is or how other students are doing.

This will help the student feel more empowered and less helpless in the face of their struggles. They can take action where they can and accept the things they cannot change. By focusing on what they can control, they can increase their chances of success and feel more confident in their abilities.

NONJUDGMENTAL THINKING

Nonjudgmental thinking is the act of observing and recognizing one's thoughts without attaching any labels or opinions to them. This mental state is important in letting go because it allows people to view their experiences objectively and without bias. Without nonjudgmental thinking, they may hold on to negative thoughts or emotions, creating unnecessary stress and anxiety.

Nonjudgmental thinking also enables people to accept their thoughts and feelings without shame or guilt, allowing them to move forward and let go of any negative or limiting beliefs. By cultivating a nonjudgmental mindset, they can gain a deeper understanding of themselves and the world around them, ultimately leading them to a more peaceful and fulfilling life.

Nonjudgmental thinking is an essential component of letting go. It involves the ability to observe and acknowledge one's thoughts and feelings without labeling them as good or bad. At times, judgmental thoughts can keep people stuck in a cycle of negative emotions and prevent them from moving forward. For instance, consider that an individual made a mistake at their job, and their boss criticized their work. Instead of judging themself by stating that they are a failure or that they are incompetent, they can try to observe their thoughts and emotions with kindness and understanding. Doing so can help them see the situation more objectively and move past the negative emotions, which can hinder their progress.

In essence, nonjudgmental thinking helps people adopt a more compassionate and accepting attitude toward themselves and others, which is vital in the process of letting go.

As part of their mindfulness training, individuals participating in dialectical behavior therapy (DBT) skills groups are taught how to think without making judgments. The practice of mindfulness helps individuals watch and describe their own actions, which is especially important when learning a new behavior, addressing a problem, or recognizing the need for change and letting go of the past. This practice helps individuals more fully engage in their lives without being weighed down by preconceived notions or biases. The ultimate goal is to cultivate a *nonjudgmental stance*, which means that individuals learn to recognize and accept things as they are, without labeling them as good or bad. In essence, the focus is on understanding and accepting the facts, rather than applying subjective judgments or opinions.

By practicing mindfulness and developing a nonjudgmental stance, individuals can experience greater emotional stability and resilience, which can help them to better manage stress, regulate their emotions, and improve their relationships with others (Hoge et al., 2013). Additionally, by developing a deeper understanding and acceptance of the present moment, individuals may be better equipped to make positive changes in their lives and work toward their personal goals (Chambers et al., 2008).

The concept of judgment is often used to express one's preferences or opinions, but it can also be a quick and sometimes inaccurate interpretation of people's surroundings that influences their thoughts and behaviors. People's judgments are based on their own experiences and are not necessarily objective facts.

For example, when people say that they find a piece of clothing pretty or beautiful, they are expressing their personal preference for it. Conversely, if they say that something is ugly, they are indicating that they do not like it. However, the problem arises when people forget that their opinions and preferences are subjective and may not necessarily reflect reality.

While making decisions is a natural part of life, it is important to be aware of one's own judgmental thoughts and learn how to think without judgment in order to reduce emotional reactivity. By becoming more mindful of our thoughts and avoiding hasty judgments, people can cultivate a more objective and balanced perspective on the world around them. This can lead to greater emotional regulation, increased self-awareness, and more fulfilling relationships with others.

Exercises in Cultivating a Nonjudgmental Stance

Judgment into Nonjudgment

The exercise of turning judgment into nonjudgment involves rewriting negative judgments in a form that is nonjudgmental, allowing for a more objective and balanced perspective. Instead of expressing an opinion or preference, individuals aim to describe the situation factually, along with their feelings and thoughts about it.

For example, instead of saying "I hate this baby crying on the plane. Not everyone has to be a parent!" a more mindful form would be "I hear a baby crying loudly in the seat behind me. I feel angry at his parents and like they need to do a better job. But maybe it's not in their control? Babies have a mind of their own, and there's only so much they can do. But I have to acknowledge that I am feeling irritated and angry." By reframing one's judgment in this way, people can acknowledge our feelings without directing blame or negativity toward others.

Similarly, instead of saying "My boyfriend is so selfish. I hate him! What a jerk! He only thinks about himself! He always forgets the plans we make," a more mindful form would be "My boyfriend forgot about the plan we made today. He doesn't always do that, though. I feel angry and like I want to have an argument with him. I am thinking that he only thinks about himself (but that is not true)." In this example, the person adds a reality check to their thoughts, recognizing that their initial judgment may not be entirely accurate.

By practicing this exercise, people can learn to recognize and reframe their judgments, allowing them to view situations in a more objective and compassionate manner. For instance, instead of saying "The stupid driver in front me obviously doesn't know how to drive! Who does he think he is, cutting me off!" people can say "The person in front of me is driving very fast and cut across my lane. I feel unsafe. This whole situation makes me feel enraged." By describing the situation factually and acknowledging one's own emotions without directing blame or judgment toward others, individuals can cultivate greater empathy and understanding in their daily lives. Here's another example to help solidify this concept:

Once upon a time, there lived an optimistic young woman who had a habit of judging herself harshly. She was very talented in many ways, yet she would often put herself down instead of celebrating her successes. She'd start sentences with "I should have done better" or "It's all my fault," without even pausing to consider the circumstances or other factors that may have contributed to any given situation.

One day, this young woman decided enough was enough—it was time for a change! She knew that if she wanted to break free from her self-judgmental habits, she needed to start reframing her negative self-talk into something more realistic and positive.

The young woman began by taking note of what triggered these negative thoughts— usually when things weren't going as planned or when someone else said something hurtful about her. Then, instead of letting those words consume her thoughts and make them spiral downward, she made an effort to take a step back and look at each situation objectively, assessing what went wrong (if anything), but also looking at the bigger picture. This helped put everything into perspective so that while mistakes were acknowledged, they no longer seemed like such huge failures anymore because they were seen in light of everything else that had gone right up until then.

Next came changing how she spoke to herself: replacing harsh judgments with kinder affirmations like "I can learn from this experience" or "I'm doing my best," which not only boosted her confidence but also encouraged resilience whenever faced with adversity again in future scenarios. Most importantly, though? It allowed the young woman to feel proud for giving it her all regardless of whether things worked out—a key factor toward realizing true contentment within oneself rather than constantly striving after success alone as validation for one's worthiness as a human being.

The moral behind this story is simple: Judgment does nothing productive for individuals unless they use it wisely, so why not learn how to turn one's own judgment into nonjudgment by reframing their negative self-talk into something more realistic and positive? After all, life is much brighter on the other side!

Repetitive Judgments

Repetitive judgments are judgments that people constantly make about themselves, others, or situations. These judgments can be negative and can create negative feelings and behaviors. The exercise of addressing repetitive judgments involves three steps: describing the judgment objectively, identifying how the judgment makes us feel, and imagining what life would look like without this judgment.

The first step is to describe the judgment objectively, without any negative or judgmental language. For example, if someone constantly judges themselves for not being able to quit smoking, they might write: "I have been smoking for two years now, and I usually tend to label myself with offensive words because I haven't managed to quit yet. I have this bad habit, and I know that it is harmful for my health." By describing the situation factually, individuals can gain a clearer understanding of the situation and begin to recognize the negative judgments they make.

The second step is to identify how the judgment makes them feel. Negative judgments often produce negative feelings, which can reinforce negative behaviors. For example, after judging oneself for not being able to quit smoking, one might feel self-hatred and depressed, which can lead to increased smoking and further reinforce negative beliefs about oneself. By identifying these feelings, people can begin to recognize the negative impact of their judgments and start to address them.

The third step is to imagine what life would look like without this judgment. This step involves considering how things might be different if they did not make this judgment. For example, if someone could imagine not judging themselves for their smoking habit, they might feel more at ease and be more motivated to try new approaches to quitting smoking. By imagining a different reality, individuals can begin to see new possibilities and potential solutions. For example:

Negative judgment: *"I'm always so disorganized and messy. I'll never be able to keep my space clean and tidy."*

Step 1: Describe the judgment

"I often judge myself for being disorganized and messy. I tend to label myself negatively and feel like I'll never be able to keep my space clean and tidy."

Step 2: How I feel about the judgment
"Whenever I make this judgment, I feel overwhelmed and frustrated. I also feel like I'm not good enough or capable of achieving what I want. This negative self-talk just makes me feel worse and less motivated to take action."

Step 3: What life would look like without this judgment
"If I could let go of this judgment and negative self-talk, I might feel more at ease and motivated to make changes. I could focus on taking small steps toward organizing my space, instead of feeling overwhelmed by the idea of being perfectly clean and tidy. By recognizing my progress and celebrating small victories, I might feel more positive and capable of achieving my goal."

By applying the exercise of addressing repetitive judgments, individuals can become more aware of their negative self-talk and learn to cultivate a more positive and compassionate mindset. By describing the judgment objectively, identifying how it makes one feel, and imagining a different reality without it, people can begin to challenge their negative beliefs and behaviors and cultivate a greater sense of self-acceptance and confidence. Here's an illustrative example:

Alice had been struggling with the same judgment for as long as she could remember. It followed her everywhere like an invisible shadow, and it seemed to be rooted in a deep-seated insecurity—"I will never have the courage or the bravery to pursue my dream of becoming a singer." Every time she tried something new or stepped outside her comfort zone, this judgment would rear its ugly head and start murmuring negative thoughts about how Alice wasn't good enough or capable enough to do what she wanted.

The repetitive judgments weighed heavily on Alice's heart and mind. She felt frustrated and discouraged by them, wondering why they kept popping up when all she wanted to do was live her life without fear or self-doubt holding her back.

One day, while trying to find a way out of this vicious cycle of negativity, Alice stopped and asked herself "What if I didn't have these judgments? What if I actually allowed myself to let go of them and try things without worrying about being judged?" The thought made her feel lighter instantly—suddenly there was hope that maybe she could break free from these shackles that had been weighing down on her for so long!

Alice decided then and there that from now on, whenever those negative thoughts bubbled up inside her mind, instead of listening to them, she would take a deep breath and focus on the positive possibilities ahead of her instead. She would think about what life could look like without the judgments clouding it over—full of courage, possibility, and joy!

This newfound sense of freedom gave Alice strength; no longer did those negative judgments define who she was or limit what she could achieve—instead they became just another part of the journey toward becoming more confident in herself than ever before! By addressing repetitive judgments and identifying how they made her feel, and imagining a different reality without them, she became more aware of her judgments and their impact on her feelings and behaviors, which ended up helping her in cultivating a more positive and compassionate mindset.

SELF-DISTANCING

Psychological distancing, or more commonly known as self-distancing, refers to the ability to step back and create space between oneself and a source of strong emotions or conflict. It involves taking a more objective perspective on a situation and reflecting on one's course of action rather than being immediately dominated by emotions or impulses. The ability to engage in psychological distancing is an important skill that can help individuals regulate their emotions, let go of the past, improve decision-making, and reduce the negative impact of stress on mental health.

One way that psychological distancing can be beneficial is by helping individuals gain a clearer perspective on a situation (König et al., 2017). By creating space between oneself and a source of conflict, individuals can reflect on the situation from a more objective standpoint and gain a more comprehensive understanding of the factors contributing to the conflict. This increased understanding can facilitate effective problem-solving, negotiation, and conflict resolution.

In addition to facilitating problem-solving, psychological distancing can also promote creativity. Förster et al. (2004) found that people who were asked to think about a problem from a long-term, abstract perspective were more likely to generate creative solutions compared to those who were asked to think about the problem from a short-term, concrete perspective. The authors suggest that the act of mentally distancing oneself from the immediate context of a problem can enhance creativity by allowing for more abstract and flexible thinking.

By taking a step back from a concrete problem and approaching it from a more abstract perspective, individuals can identify novel and innovative solutions that might not have been apparent from a narrower perspective. This can be particularly helpful in situations where individuals feel stuck or overwhelmed, as it allows them to approach the problem with a fresh perspective and generate new ideas.

Another benefit of psychological distancing is its ability to promote emotion regulation (Kross, 2017). By creating space between oneself and a source of strong emotions, individuals can better regulate their emotional responses and engage in more adaptive coping strategies. This can be particularly important in situations where individuals are facing high levels of stress or anxiety, as it can reduce the negative impact of stress on mental health.

Overall, the ability to engage in psychological distancing is an important skill that can facilitate effective problem-solving, promote creativity, and improve emotional regulation. By creating space between oneself and a source of conflict or strong emotions, individuals can gain a clearer perspective on the situation, let go of painful thoughts, and make more thoughtful and effective decisions. When used in a healthy and appropriate manner, psychological distancing can facilitate healthy self-distancing and promote the ability to let go of negative experiences.

Healthy self-distancing involves taking an observer's perspective on one's own thoughts, feelings, and behaviors in order to gain greater self-awareness and insight. By creating psychological distance between oneself and one's experiences, individuals can gain a more objective and reflective perspective on their own internal processes. This can facilitate greater self-awareness, help individuals identify patterns of behavior or thought that may be causing distress, and promote insight into one's own values, goals, and motivations.

Psychological distancing can also promote the ability to let go of negative experiences (Kross, 2012). By creating space between oneself and a source of conflict or strong emotions, individuals can gain a more reflective perspective on the situation and identify strategies for moving forward. This can involve reframing the situation in a more positive light, focusing on the aspects of the situation that are within one's control, or identifying new strategies for coping with difficult emotions or experiences. By letting go of negative experiences in this way, individuals can promote greater resilience, reduce the impact of stress on mental health, and cultivate a more positive outlook on life. Consider this illustrative example:

Kiara is feeling overwhelmed and anxious. She has been dealing with a lot lately, including work stress, family drama, and financial struggles. With so much on her plate, she feels like she can't see the whole picture of her life or make any rational decisions about what to do next.

That's when Kiara hears about psychological distance—an approach that could help her take a step back from her situation and gain clarity on what needs to be done. Remember, psychological distance is all about creating mental space between yourself and the problem by looking at it objectively rather than emotionally.

So Kiara decides to give it a go. She imagines herself in an aeroplane flying high above her problems below—with enough perspective to get some insight into how insignificant they actually are in comparison to the bigger picture of life. As she looks down at everything going on below, suddenly things don't seem as serious anymore; even though there are still many challenges ahead of her, she now realizes that all these events will eventually pass away, too, while other new ones will come up instead—just like clouds moving across the sky each day!

Gaining this newfound perspective through psychological distance allows Kiara to remain calm amidst all the chaos in her life. For once she is able to think clearly about how to best tackle all of these issues one by one without getting bogged down by their cumulative weight anymore!

Techniques for Self-Distancing

One effective technique for self-distancing is to *take a break and gain actual physical or temporal distance from the situation.* This can involve taking a short break of fifteen minutes or leaving the space entirely in order to be alone and gain a more reflective perspective on the situation. By stepping out of the current situation and disrupting the immediate intensity, individuals can reframe the situation and gain greater perspective. For example, if individuals are engaged in an emotionally charged argument with another person, taking a break and gaining distance can allow them to reflect on their own thoughts, feelings, and behaviors in a more objective and reflective manner. This can promote greater self-awareness, insight, and empathy, and help individuals identify strategies for resolving the conflict in a more constructive and adaptive manner.

Self-distancing will engage individuals in cognitive reappraisal. This involves reinterpreting a situation in a more positive or neutral light, and can be particularly useful in situations where individuals are experiencing negative emotions or stress. For example, if an individual is facing a difficult challenge or setback, they may try to reinterpret the situation as an opportunity for growth or learning rather than a failure or setback. This can help them reframe the situation in a more positive and constructive manner and promote greater resilience and well-being.

Let's say Danny is in a heated argument with his boss over a disagreement about a project. The argument is becoming increasingly tense, and both Danny and his boss are becoming more and more emotional. In this situation, Danny could use the technique of taking a break and gaining physical distance to promote self-distancing and gain greater perspective on the situation. He could excuse himself from the conversation and take a short break, either by leaving the room or going for a short walk outside.

During this break, Danny could reflect on his own thoughts, feelings, and behaviors in a more objective and reflective manner. He could try to identify his own emotional triggers and reactions, as well as those of his boss. He could also consider alternative interpretations of the situation and try to reframe the conflict in a more positive or constructive light.

One way to practice self-distancing is to use language that reflects a third-person perspective, such as referring to oneself by name or using "he/she/they" instead of "I/me/my." For example, instead of saying "I am feeling anxious," Danny can say " Danny is feeling anxious." This simple change in language can help to create mental distance between John and his feelings, allowing him to reflect on them more objectively.

By taking a break and gaining physical distance, Danny would be able to regulate his emotional responses and engage in more adaptive coping strategies. He would also be able to promote greater self-awareness and insight, and identify strategies for resolving the conflict in a more constructive and adaptive manner.

The Eisenhower matrix is a powerful technique for self-distancing that can be used to gain greater perspective and prioritize tasks. This technique involves creating a two by two matrix with the columns Urgent and Less Urgent and the rows Important and Less Important. Tasks are then assigned to one of the cells within this matrix based on their level of urgency and importance. The Urgent-Important quadrant includes tasks that are both urgent and important, such as a deadline that is fast approaching. These tasks require immediate attention and should be prioritized.

The Less Urgent-Important quadrant includes tasks that are important but not urgent, such as long-term projects or personal development goals. These tasks are important for personal growth and development, but can be planned for and completed over a longer period of time. The Urgent-Less Important quadrant includes tasks that are urgent but not important, such as responding to nonessential emails or attending unnecessary meetings. These tasks can often be delegated or postponed in order to focus on more important tasks.

The Less Urgent-Less Important quadrant includes tasks that are neither urgent nor important, such as social media browsing or other time-wasting activities. These tasks should be minimized or eliminated in order to focus on more important tasks.

For example, consider Arthur, who is a business owner who is feeling overwhelmed with his workload. He decides to use the Eisenhower matrix to gain greater perspective and prioritize his tasks. After assigning each task to a quadrant within the matrix, Arthur realizes that he has been spending too much time on tasks in the Urgent-Less Important quadrant, such as responding to nonessential emails. He decides to delegate some of these tasks to his assistant and focus more on tasks in the Urgent-Important quadrant, such as meeting upcoming deadlines. He also decides to prioritize tasks in the Less Urgent-Important quadrant, such as working on long-term projects and personal development goals. By using the Eisenhower matrix, Arthur is able to gain greater perspective and prioritize his tasks more effectively, reducing his feelings of overwhelm and stress.

The technique of watching yourself from a distance is a self-distancing technique that involves changing the focus of one's perspective from a first-person view to a third-person view. By imagining that one is watching themselves from a distance, individuals can suspend some of the immediate emotional and psychological reactions that they might be experiencing in an emotionally charged situation.

This technique can help them reconsider their behavior as if they are observing someone else in their position. By doing so, they can gain a more objective perspective on the situation and their behavior, which can help them in making more deliberate and effective choices.

For example, let's say Sarah is in a heated argument with her partner. In the heat of the moment, she is feeling angry and defensive, and her emotions are clouding her judgment. To apply the technique of watching herself from a distance, she imagines that she is watching the argument from a third-person perspective, as if she were observing someone else in the same situation.

To practice self-distancing, Sarah can start by taking a deep breath and consciously shifting her attention away from her own thoughts and feelings. She can then try to mentally place herself in the position of an objective observer who is watching the argument unfold from a distance. She can imagine what it would be like to watch two people arguing without being directly involved in the conflict.

Sarah can also try using language that reflects a third-person perspective, just like John in the previous case. For example, instead of saying "I am so angry right now," she can say "Sarah is feeling angry." This simple change in language can help create mental distance between herself and her feelings, allowing her to observe the situation more objectively.

From this perspective, Sarah is able to see that her partner is also feeling hurt and upset, and that both of them are contributing to the conflict. She is able to suspend some of her immediate emotional reactions and take a more objective view of the situation. This allows her to consider her behavior and communication more carefully, and to make more deliberate choices that can help de-escalate the conflict and move toward resolution.

By using the technique of watching herself from a distance, Sarah is able to gain a more objective perspective on the situation and her behavior, which helps her make more effective choices in an emotionally charged situation.

The technique of watching yourself from the future is a powerful tool for self-distancing that can be used in various situations, such as when individuals find themselves in an emotionally charged situation or when they need to make decisions that will impact their future. This technique involves imagining oneself as "*future you*" looking back and observing one's current behavior.

To use this technique, people need to imagine themselves at some point in the future, looking back on their current behavior. They should ask themselves how they would perceive their current behavior in that future context. If they find that their current behavior is not in line with their future goals or values, they can use that realization to motivate themselves to change their behavior. Consider the following example:

For many people, it's hard to imagine competing in front of a large crowd, let alone at the Olympics. But has one ever wondered what goes through an athlete's mind right before they compete? Even with intense training, athletes still experience feelings of nervousness and anxiety before they step onto the field. And while it might seem natural to picture the worst-case scenario, successful athletes know that this type of visualization can be detrimental to their performance. It's said that visualizing a mistake, such as falling or missing a critical shot, increases the chances of the athlete actually making that mistake during the competition.

This is where the technique of watching *yourself* from the future is particularly relevant to athletes who need to perform under pressure. By imagining themselves as "future you" looking back on their current behavior, athletes can gain a broader perspective on the situation and its consequences, rather than solely focusing on immediate concrete characteristics of the competition. They can ask themselves how they would perceive their current behavior in that future context and whether it's in line with their future goals or values. This realization can motivate them to change their behavior, adopt a positive mindset, and focus on visualizing success rather than failure. By using this technique, athletes can improve their mental preparation, boost their confidence, and increase their chances of success in the competition. So, the next time you watch an Olympic athlete, remember that their mental game is just as important as their physical skills.

Another example could be Andrew's unnecessary spending. He wants to curb unnecessary spending so that he can save for a long-term goal, such as a vacation to the Maldives. However, he finds himself frequently making impulsive purchases, such as new clothing and video games. To apply the technique of watching himself from the future, Andrew imagines himself at the time of his vacation, looking back on his spending habits. From that future perspective, he realizes that his current spending is not aligned with his goal of saving for the vacation. This realization helps him resist the temptation to make impulsive purchases and instead prioritize his long-term goal.

By using the technique of watching himself from the future, Andrew is able to create temporal space and gain a broader perspective on his behavior, which enables him to make more deliberate choices that align with his values and goals.

Chapter Takeaways

- Letting go is often used in psychology to describe the process of releasing attachment to something or someone. It may refer to letting go of negative thoughts, emotions, or behaviors that hold an individual back from reaching their full potential.
- The dichotomy of control is a central concept in Stoic philosophy that

emphasizes the importance of distinguishing between things that are within one's control and things that are beyond one's control.

- One essential component of the Stoic philosophy's dichotomy of control involves developing an unwavering concentration on the present moment. This involves instructing one's mind to remain wholly involved in the current experience, rather than being sidetracked by concerns or remorse about the past, or concerns or anticipation for the future.

- Nonjudgmental thinking is the practice of acknowledging and identifying one's thoughts without affixing any characterizations or viewpoints to them. This mindset is crucial when it comes to letting go, as it empowers individuals to look at their experiences objectively and without any partiality.

- Psychological distancing, also called self-distancing, pertains to the capability of creating distance between oneself and the cause of intense emotions or conflict. This involves adopting a more impartial outlook on a circumstance and thinking about one's choices instead of being swiftly swayed by emotions or urges.

Chapter 2: Breaking the Chains of Negativity

Human beings tend to be their own harshest critics, constantly berating themselves for their perceived shortcomings and mistakes. This chapter will explore the powerful concept of breaking the chains of negativity. By doing so, people can learn to let go of their inner critic and the negativity it breeds. Changing one's mentality from perfectionism to excellentism can make all the difference in one's life. Additionally, practicing nonattachment and curating one's media consumption are two other tools people can use to break free from negative thought patterns. So hurry and start this journey of self-discovery while learning how to break free from the chains of negativity.

LETTING GO OF YOUR INNER CRITIC

Many are all too familiar with that little nagging voice in their heads that seems to only spout criticism and negative thoughts. This internal monologue can take many different forms, from scolding one for a mistake one made to questioning why they can't seem to get their act together. Regardless of the specifics, this voice can be a constant source of frustration and anxiety. While it's true that everyone experiences this self-talk in their own unique way, it's important to recognize that it's a perfectly normal and common aspect of the human experience. By learning to better understand and manage one's inner critic, people can cultivate greater self-compassion, let go of negative ruminations, and approach the world with a healthier mindset.

The concept of the inner critic is a widely recognized phenomenon in the field of psychology. It refers to the negative voice that many of us have in our heads that judges, shames, and criticizes us for our perceived flaws and shortcomings. This inner voice can be particularly loud during moments of vulnerability and can be a major barrier to personal growth and development.

Cultural norms often reinforce the belief that feedback given in the form of criticism and guilt-inducing comments will motivate behavior. However, the idea that negative reinforcement leads to positive change has been disputed by experts. When someone is criticized, the result can often lead to increased feelings of shame, fear, and resentment (Baumeister, 1995) Although it can give individuals a sense of control, these types of comments can lead to a negative cycle of self-doubt and criticism. Even when people use these thoughts with themselves, it can further perpetuate their "inner critic" and leave them feeling stuck. It's important to recognize the detrimental effects of harsh criticism and instead strive for constructive feedback that leads to positive growth and development.

Despite one's best efforts, everyone has that little voice inside their heads that tells them they are not good enough—their inner critic. It's that nagging feeling that one is not smart enough, not talented enough, not thin enough, not successful enough, and so on. The inner critic can be harsh and unforgiving, and it can hold people back from achieving their goals and living their best lives. Whether it's comparing themselves to others or feeling like an imposter, the inner critic can be a constant source of anxiety and self-doubt. But the good news is that by recognizing and challenging one's inner critic, people can learn to silence it and live more confident, fulfilling lives.

When people receive communication from their brain that triggers feelings of shame and anxiety, their natural response is to avoid it. This avoidance may seem like a short-term solution to ease one's discomfort and reduce anxiety. However, avoidant behavior does not lead to any positive change or motivation. Instead, it can manifest as procrastination, overeating, excessively watching TV, or constantly checking your phone. These behaviors can even go as far as avoiding the source of what is causing them discomfort, such as people, places, or activities. The key to moving past this avoidance cycle is to recognize it as a coping mechanism and to actively choose to engage with what makes us uncomfortable—only then can people truly motivate themselves to change.

Shame can be a debilitating feeling that can leave one feeling alone and disconnected from others. Even receiving messages from others that shame, such as "*you're not good enough*," can make people feel like they don't deserve to be a part of a community. As social creatures, humans crave connection with others, but shame can physically make them want to withdraw and avoid interactions. This avoidance can lead to a vicious cycle of self-criticism and further avoidance behaviors, ultimately keeping them from taking care of themselves and finding comfort and motivation. This is exactly what happens when one's inner critic decides to put one on blast. Learning to recognize and address these feelings of shame and self-criticism is essential for one's overall well-being and ability to connect with others.

One way to address the influence of the inner critic is to focus on the application of wisdom, strength, and love. This approach involves developing an awareness of the origins and impact of the inner critic and taking proactive steps to disengage from its negative influence. Wisdom refers to the ability to recognize the difference between the voice of the inner critic and one's own true self. This involves developing the skill of mindfulness and learning to observe one's thoughts without judgment. Through the practice of mindfulness, people can learn to recognize when the inner critic is present and begin to challenge its negative messages.

Strength refers to the ability to stand up to the inner critic. This involves developing the capacity to recognize one's own strengths and accomplishments and to take pride in one's successes. By focusing on strengths, people can begin to counteract the negative influence of the inner critic and build their self-esteem.

Love refers to the ability to be kind and compassionate toward oneself, even in the face of perceived flaws and shortcomings. This involves developing the practice of self-compassion—treating oneself with the same kindness, caring, and understanding that someone would offer to a good friend. By cultivating self-compassion, people can begin to counteract the harsh and critical voice of the inner critic and learn to accept themselves for who they are.

To illustrate this approach, consider the example of a person who struggles with social anxiety. The inner critic may tell this person that they are not good enough, that others will judge them, and that they should avoid social situations altogether. By applying the principles of wisdom, strength, and love, this person can learn to recognize the voice of the inner critic and challenge its negative messages. They can focus on their strengths, such as their ability to connect with others or their sense of humour, and use these strengths to build their self-esteem. They can also cultivate self-compassion and be kind to themselves, even when they feel anxious or uncomfortable in social situations.

In summary, the inner critic can be a major barrier to personal growth and development. By focusing on the principles of wisdom, strength, and love, people can learn to recognize the voice of the inner critic, challenge its negative messages, and cultivate a more positive and compassionate relationship with themselves.

Steps to Let Go of Your Inner Critic

Awareness is the first step toward identifying one's inner critic and letting go of it. One of the first steps in overcoming the influence of the inner critic is to become aware of its presence and its impact on one's thoughts and feelings. Many people are not even aware of the inner critic or its negative influence on their lives. Therefore, it is crucial to develop the skill of self-awareness and identify the voice of the inner critic when it arises.

The next step is to identify the situation that may have triggered the inner critic. This could be a particular event, interaction with someone, or even a thought or memory. It is important to remember that the inner critic is often triggered by situations that are perceived as threatening or challenging. Once individuals have identified the situation, they can start to explore their authentic feelings about it.

This is where the inner critic can be most helpful. By asking oneself, "What am I afraid of? What would it mean if that happened? And what would that mean?" people can begin to dig deeper and uncover their most vulnerable feelings about the situation. Often, the inner critic is trying to protect people from feeling these vulnerable emotions, such as fear, shame, or rejection.

However, it is important to recognize that individuals can handle these emotions and that they are a natural part of the human experience. By allowing themselves the space to feel these emotions, people can start to let go of the protective mechanisms of the inner critic and develop a more positive and compassionate relationship with themselves.

In summary, becoming aware of the presence and impact of the inner critic is the first step in overcoming its negative influence. By identifying the situations that trigger the inner critic and exploring one's authentic feelings about them, people can begin to let go of the protective mechanisms of the inner critic and develop a more positive and compassionate relationship with themselves.

Here's an example:

Ian is a high school student who has always been passionate about playing basketball. However, he recently had a few bad games and missed several important shots. After one particularly rough game, he started to hear the voice of his inner critic saying, "You're not good enough. You'll never be good enough. You're letting down your team and your coach."

What is he afraid of? Ian is afraid of failing and letting down his team and coach. He may also be afraid of not being good enough to achieve his dreams of playing college basketball or beyond. What authentic feelings might he be having about this situation that aren't related to shame triggers? What are his vulnerabilities? (Identify your vulnerability and feel those feelings.)

Ian says, "I feel disappointed, frustrated, and overwhelmed. Basketball has always been important to me, and I don't know what I would do if I wasn't good at it. I also feel pressure to live up to my own expectations and those of others."

What does he really need? Ian says, "I need to remember why I love basketball and focus on improving my skills rather than just winning. I also need to give myself permission to make mistakes and learn from them. And most importantly, I need to be kind and compassionate toward myself, even when I don't meet my own expectations."

Here individuals need to ask themselves "What are some self-criticisms that you are aware of hearing yourself say? What self-criticisms are you aware of hearing yourself express?" By identifying these negative thoughts using the second-person perspective, people can begin to challenge their validity and develop a more positive and compassionate relationship with themselves.

For example, one self-criticism that someone may be aware of hearing themselves say is "*I am not good enough*" *or "I am not worthy of love."* This negative thought can be particularly damaging because it can impact many different areas of a person's life, from their relationships to their career to their personal goals. Another self-criticism may be, "*I always mess things up.*" This negative thought can lead to feelings of hopelessness and a sense of being stuck in a cycle of failure and disappointment.

Another example of a self-criticism that someone may be aware of hearing themselves express is "I am such a coward. I am contemptible and useless. Be cautious, or you will get injured. I must exert more effort." This negative self-talk using first-person pronouns can be particularly damaging because it not only criticizes the person's actions but also attacks their character and worth as a person. Now consider the below example:

Janine has a tendency to engage in negative self-talk, and often criticizes herself for her perceived shortcomings. For instance, when she makes a mistake at work, she might say to herself, "I'm so stupid. I can't believe I messed up again. I'm never going to be successful at my job."

By using the second-person perspective, Janine could reframe her self-criticism into more compassionate and supportive self-talk. For example, instead of saying "I'm so stupid," she could say "You made a mistake, but everyone makes mistakes. It's okay to not be perfect." This way, Janine is speaking to herself in a kind and empathetic manner, rather than being harsh and critical. By practicing this type of self-talk, she can develop greater self-compassion and improve her emotional well-being. She may also find that she is better able to cope with setbacks and challenges, as she is not being held back by negative self-judgment.

Next, individuals need to connect with that sentiment. Fear is a natural emotion that can be triggered by any number of scenarios. Whether it's a fear of spiders, heights, or public speaking, there's always something that sends shivers down one's spine. But people seldom ever stop to consider what lies beyond the fear itself. When people experience fears or anxieties, it can often be accompanied by a host of other genuine emotions, such as sadness, frustration, or even anger. It's important to recognize these emotions as separate from any potential shame triggers, and to give oneself the space and understanding to work through them. By acknowledging and connecting with these emotions, people can better understand the root of their fears and take steps toward overcoming them and letting them go.

Many people have a tendency to be self-critical, often saying hurtful things to themselves like "You're such a coward" or "You're worthless." But how does it feel to hear those things? Take a moment to really tap into those emotions—"What are you afraid of, and what authentic feelings are you experiencing that aren't related to shame triggers?" It's important to recognize that there are opposing feelings as well, and reactions to these self-criticisms. *So, what do you say to that voice that tells you you're useless?* It's time to start reframing those negative self-talk patterns and instead focus on more positive and uplifting thoughts.

Hearing these self-criticisms may evoke negative emotions such as shame, guilt, or anger. By getting in touch with these feelings, someone can begin to explore what may be triggering their negative self-talk.

They may be afraid of feeling vulnerable or exposed, or they may fear the consequences of not living up to their own or others' expectations. Some authentic feelings they may be having about this situation that aren't related to shame triggers might include frustration, disappointment, or a sense of being overwhelmed. They may feel like they are not making progress toward their goals or that they are not living up to their potential.

Some opposite feelings may include self-compassion, self-acceptance, and self-love. These feelings can be nurtured by focusing on positive affirmations and building a sense of self-worth based on one's strengths and accomplishments. Reactions to these opposite feelings may include feeling more motivated and inspired to take positive steps toward their goals. They may feel more confident in their abilities and more willing to take risks and try new things.

When that voice says they are useless, they can respond by challenging that thought and replacing it with a more positive and affirming message. For example, they could say "I am not useless. I have many strengths and accomplishments that make me a valuable person." By practicing positive self-talk and affirmations, they can begin to shift their internal dialogue toward a more positive and compassionate voice.

Express empathy for the inner critic's fear and out-of-control feelings. When people hear their inner critic start to criticize them or cause them to spiral into negative thought patterns, it's easy to get lost in those emotions. However, it's important to remember that the inner critic is often trying to protect them from past hurts and rejections. When individuals show empathy toward their inner critic, they can acknowledge its fears and out-of-control feelings without allowing them to take over.

By saying things like "I understand where you're coming from" or "I know you're doing this to protect me," people can separate themselves from the negative thoughts and shift their focus toward self-compassion. Though it may take practice and patience, expressing empathy toward the inner critic can help people break free from those harmful thought patterns and move toward a more positive and confident mindset.

When one expresses their reaction to their inner critic's negative self-talk, they take an active step toward breaking free from its grip on their thoughts and emotions. By acknowledging that the critical voice is not helpful and requesting that it stop, they begin to take control of their inner dialogue.

It is important to remind oneself that they will be okay and able to cope with whatever happens. This helps to counteract the fear and anxiety that the inner critic often instills. By emphasizing the fact that they do not need to be afraid, they empower themselves to take action and move forward. For example, if one is feeling anxious or overwhelmed, they might say to themselves,

"It's understandable that you're feeling this way. These feelings are valid and important."

Express your reaction. Finally, it is essential to recognize and address one's genuine needs. In this case, the need to feel connected to others. By reminding themselves of this need, they can focus their attention on building meaningful relationships and connections with others. This can help them feel less isolated and more supported, which can, in turn, reduce the power of the inner critic's negative self-talk. Consider the following example that illustrates all the steps of letting go of one's inner critic:

Let's take the example of Jess, who has been struggling with anxiety and negative self-talk from her inner critic. Jess often feels overwhelmed and nervous, and her inner critic tends to tell her that she is not good enough, that she will fail, and that she should avoid taking risks.

To start, Jess becomes aware of her negative self-talk and recognizes that it is coming from her inner critic. She begins to pay attention to her thoughts and feelings, noticing when the critical voice starts to chime in. She also takes note of the situations or triggers that tend to set off her inner critic, such as social situations or work-related tasks.

Next, Jess takes a moment to connect with her emotions and determine her genuine feelings toward these situations. She recognizes that her fear of failure is a big driver behind her inner critic's negative self-talk. She also realizes that what she really needs is to feel more confident and supported, rather than constantly questioning herself and doubting her abilities.

With this in mind, Jess begins to speak to her inner critic using third-person pronouns. She expresses empathy for her inner critic's fear and anxiety by saying something like, "I know you're feeling scared and unsure right now, but I'm here to tell you that I'm okay. I'm capable of handling whatever comes my way."

She then expresses her reaction to the negative self-talk by saying something like, "Your critical voice is not helping me right now. It's preventing me from feeling confident and connected to others. I need you to stop talking to me this way."

Finally, Jess reminds herself of what she truly needs by expressing herself. "What I really need is to feel supported and connected to others. I don't have to be afraid of failing or making mistakes. I'm worthy of love and acceptance just as I am."

By speaking to her inner critic in this way, Jess is taking an active step toward breaking free from its grip on her thoughts and emotions. She is acknowledging her genuine needs and working to counteract the fear and anxiety that her inner critic tends to instill. Over time, with practice, Jess can learn to cultivate a more positive and supportive inner dialogue, one that helps her feel more confident, capable, and connected to others.

CHANGE PERFECTIONISM TO EXCELLENTISM

Individuals often find themselves stuck on a particular task or idea because of their perfectionist tendencies. Nobody is alone in experiencing this. Perfectionism can hold people back in many ways, but there's a healthy alternative: excellentism. Coined by psychology professor Patrick Gaudreau at the University of Ottawa, excellentism involves setting high standards for oneself, but not allowing those standards to become unattainable or detrimental to one's well-being. Rather than beating oneself up for missing the mark, people can choose to be open to new experiences, employ creative problem-solving, and learn from their mistakes as they continue to strive for excellence. Letting go of perfectionism doesn't mean people settle for mediocrity; it simply means they acknowledge that progress, not perfection, is what matters most.

The pursuit of perfection is a double-edged sword. On one hand, aiming for the highest level of excellence can motivate people to work harder and strive for the best. On the other hand, when perfectionists set unrealistic standards for themselves, they set themselves up for failure. No one is perfect, and expecting flawless performances every time is not only unsustainable but also damaging to one's mental health and self-esteem. As a result, when people fall short of their expectations, the self-criticism and harsh judgment that follow can weigh heavily on them and prevent them from letting go and bouncing back from setbacks. It's important to recognize that progress is not always linear, and that celebrating small victories and learning from mistakes is essential for growth and self-improvement.

Individuals are often praised for their perfectionism and drive to succeed in everything they do. From a young age, people are encouraged to strive for excellence, whether it be in academics, sports, or even their appearance. However, this pursuit of perfection can quickly become a slippery slope, as it can lead to unrealistic expectations and a constant need to outdo themselves. The pressure to maintain the highest standards can be overwhelming, and it's easy to get caught up in the cycle of always trying to achieve more. As a result, people may be vulnerable to the pitfalls of perfectionism. It's important to remember that perfection is not attainable, nor is it necessary for success. Instead, people should focus on doing their best and celebrating their achievements, no matter how big or small.

Perfectionism has long been lauded as a positive trait, but research shows that it can actually be harmful. The pressure to be flawless can lead to mental health issues like anxiety and depression, as well as low self-worth (Stoeber, 2014). Perfectionists may also struggle to handle failure, as the stakes are often so incredibly high in their minds. This can lead to procrastination and avoidance, which can ultimately impact their success. In fact, some perfectionists may even stop taking on challenges altogether because the fear of failure is simply too great. As such, it's clear that perfectionism is not the path to success that many think it is.

Excellentism seems to be a more balanced approach to setting high standards for oneself without the detrimental effects of perfectionism. By focusing on excellence rather than perfection, one can still achieve their goals and maintain a positive outlook when things don't go according to plan. Embracing mistakes and learning from them can be a powerful tool for personal growth and development. It's important to keep in mind that excellence is a journey, not a destination, and that progress is more important than perfection.

Imagine a student who wants to achieve high grades in their exams. If they were a perfectionist, they might set unrealistic expectations for themselves, such as getting an A+ on every exam. If they were unable to achieve this, they might become demoralized and feel like a failure.

On the other hand, if they were an excellentist, they would still set high standards for themselves, but they would recognize that getting a perfect score every time is unlikely. Instead, they should focus on doing their best, learning from their mistakes, and striving for improvement on their next exam.

For example, if they got a B on their first exam, instead of beating themselves up over it, they would use this as an opportunity to learn from their mistakes. They would analyze what went wrong, identify areas where they need to improve, and come up with a plan to do better next time. They would also acknowledge that getting a B is still a great achievement and a step toward excellence, rather than a failure.

In essence, excellentism is about focusing on the journey toward excellence, rather than being fixated on a perfect outcome. It's about setting realistic expectations for oneself, striving for improvement, and embracing mistakes as opportunities for growth.

Being an excellentist can actually be good for one's mental health. It might sound counterintuitive, but individuals who strive for excellence often exhibit higher levels of healthy anxiety, conscientiousness, and intrinsic motivation. Not only do they make greater progress on their life goals, but they also report higher levels of positive well-being. What's even more intriguing is that they don't suffer from the negative effects of perfectionism commonly associated with high achievers, such as burnout, procrastination, and depression. So, perhaps it's worth striving for excellence after all (Stoeber & Otto, 2006).

Excellentism acknowledges that there is a limit to how much effort people can put in before they start to experience diminishing returns. It recognizes that while hard work is essential, it's not enough on its own, and that quality matters just as much as quantity.

Perfectionism can often lead people down the path of diminishing returns and even decreasing returns, where they become so fixated on achieving the perfect outcome that they lose sight of what's important. They can become less productive, less creative, and less fulfilled as a result. Excellentism, on the other hand, allows them to focus on doing their best while acknowledging that perfection is an unrealistic goal.

By setting high standards for oneself and striving for excellence, people can achieve great things while also enjoying the journey along the way. They can learn from their mistakes, grow as individuals and creatives, and become more resilient in the face of challenges. Excellentism opens people up to new experiences and allows them to approach problems in unique and creative ways, which can lead to even greater success and satisfaction.

In contrast, perfectionists can become so fixated on achieving the perfect outcome that they lose sight of the bigger picture. They can become paralyzed by the fear of making mistakes or not living up to their own impossibly high standards. This can lead to burnout, reduced productivity, and a decreased ability to adapt to changing circumstances.

Overall, excellentism is a healthier and more sustainable approach to achieving success than perfectionism. By setting high but achievable standards, being open to new experiences and approaches, and investing sufficient effort without becoming overly fixated on perfection, people can operate within the zone of increasing returns and achieve their goals efficiently and creatively.

How to Change Perfectionism to Excellentism

Individuals need to start by asking themselves a couple of questions: *"Are you a perfectionist who often finds it hard to meet your own high standards? Do you constantly hear your inner critic telling you that you're not good enough?"* It's time to change that mindset from perfectionism to excellentism. Remember, this means striving for excellence, but not letting unrealistic expectations sabotage one's efforts or take away from one's achievements. Progress is more important than perfection. By focusing on progress and continuous improvement, people can silence their inner critic and embrace a more positive and rewarding approach to life. So, next time one feels overwhelmed by expectations, they need to take a step back, reframe their mindset, and start their journey toward excellentism.

The key is to start small and focus on one area of life where one tends to get perfectionistic. Consider Orlando. For him, it's hosting. He often feels like he needs to be the perfect host, like Martha Stewart herself. But being an excellentist is not about being perfect; it's about striving for excellence. So, instead of obsessing over every detail, he focuses on the big picture and what truly matters: creating a welcoming atmosphere for his guests. By letting go of the need for perfection, Orlando can channel his energy toward creating an unforgettable experience for everyone involved. Remember, being an excellentist is not about being flawless, but about consistently striving for one's personal best.

When someone tends to be perfectionistic about a particular activity, such as hosting, they may feel like anything less than perfect is a failure. It's important to identify this behavior and acknowledge that it can be both exhausting and counterproductive. To overcome this tendency toward perfectionism, it can be helpful to make a list of what perfect looks like to *you*, as this can help people identify the specific areas where they tend to place a lot of pressure on themselves. For example, someone who is perfectionistic about hosting may list *an impeccably clean house* and *scrumptious food ready when everyone arrives* as key components of a perfect gathering.

Once an individual has their list, it's important to pick something they are willing to let go of, even if it doesn't meet their standards of perfection. This might involve accepting that the house won't be perfectly clean or allowing themselves to use ready-made side dishes from the grocery store. By practicing letting go of these things, they can observe what happens and how it affects the outcome of the activity, as well as their own feelings and the feelings of others involved.

It's important to remember that imperfection can often lead to unexpected and delightful outcomes. For example, if one is hosting a gathering and allows themself to let go of the need for a perfectly clean house, they might find that their guests feel more comfortable and at ease, and that the atmosphere is more relaxed and enjoyable. By embracing imperfection and focusing on progress rather than perfection, they can begin to overcome their tendency toward perfectionism and enjoy the activity more fully.

Additionally, practicing self-compassion is key when it comes to overcoming perfectionism. People should treat themselves with kindness and understanding, and remember that it's okay to make mistakes or fall short of their own expectations. Celebrate small victories along the way and focus on making progress, rather than striving for absolute perfection.

PRACTICING NONATTACHMENT

Practicing nonattachment can be a challenging task, but a rewarding one. Nonattachment is the practice of letting go of the need to control, cling, or possess things in life. It does not mean becoming detached or indifferent, but rather, accepting that everything in life is temporary and constantly changing. By letting go of attachment, we can experience greater freedom and less suffering. We can more easily adapt to change and find inner peace. It is important to remember that practicing nonattachment is a process and requires consistent effort. However, through this practice, people can gain a deeper understanding of themselves and the world around them.

Nonattachment is rooted in Eastern philosophy and spirituality, which suggests that people should aim to detach themselves from their desires, emotions, and material possessions. It is not about rejecting or denying these things but rather acknowledging and accepting them without clinging to them. The practice of nonattachment encourages individuals to let go of their cravings, fears, and expectations, which can cause suffering and dissatisfaction. By practicing nonattachment, individuals can develop a sense of inner peace and freedom as they become less attached to the external world.

As mentioned earlier, nonattachment can be applied to various aspects of life, including relationships. Nonattachment in relationships does not mean avoiding love or intimacy but rather being open and present in the moment without expectations or clinging to the person. It involves accepting the impermanence of relationships and allowing them to evolve naturally without attachment to any particular outcome.

Unhealthy attachment refers to the situation when individuals attach their sense of self or identity to things, relationships, and/or beliefs. Such attachment results in the fear of losing them or the desire to accumulate more, which ultimately leads to making choices based on external circumstances rather than one's inner values. Unhealthy attachment can manifest in different ways depending on the aspect of life involved.

Material attachment involves defining oneself based on possessions, such as clothes, cars, electronics, or living in a certain way. Individuals with material attachment may make poor financial decisions to maintain a particular lifestyle or work excessively to afford material possessions that they rarely get to enjoy. They may worry about their appearance, possessions, or job title and feel overwhelmed by clutter, but struggle to let go of things.

Personal attachment can be seen in people-pleasing, taking on too much work, not being able to say no, avoiding conflict, settling for negative relationships, and sacrificing one's well-being for others' demands. Individuals with personal attachment may also hold unrealistic expectations of themselves and others, define themselves through another person, and take others' behavior personally.

Beliefs attachment is characterized by perfectionism, feeling attacked when others disagree, avoiding experiences that challenge one's beliefs, refusing to consider alternatives, limiting oneself to like-minded relationships or environments, feeling intense anger when things happen outside of one's beliefs, feeling the need to get others on one's side, or holding on to stories of disempowerment. The more unhealthy attachments individuals have, the more they feel they have to lose. This leads to fear and defensiveness, causing decisions that are driven by external circumstances rather than their inner leader and core values.

The path to nonattachment involves letting go of one's identity in relation to things outside oneself and coming back to one's true self. It is a journey of self-discovery and acceptance that requires awareness, mindfulness, and the ability to let go of desires, fears, and expectations. By practicing nonattachment, individuals can experience freedom from suffering, inner peace, and a deeper connection with themselves and the world around them.

Consider Linda. She had always been a timid girl, afraid to take risks and try new things. She was content with the life she had created for herself, even if it seemed too small and mundane at times. But deep down she knew something was missing in her life; that there must be more than what she already possessed. One day Linda decided to take a leap of faith and do something brave: travel to an unfamiliar place on her own. Although scared of the unknown, Linda felt compelled to move forward with this decision as if some unseen force were guiding her every step.

When Linda arrived in the new city, everything was so different from what she was used to—from the bustling streets filled with people speaking languages other than English, to exotic flavors of food tempting her taste buds—it all seemed overwhelming yet exciting at the same time!

As Linda explored further into this strange yet fascinating place, taking in its culture and beauty along the way, she began discovering parts of herself that had remained hidden away due to fear or self-doubt and only ever being in and around a place she felt attached to. Pieces that made up who she truly was inside but that needed exploration in order to come alive again, pieces such as courage and creativity that emerged when faced with challenges outside of her comfort zone, like traveling abroad alone!

Eventually Linda found within herself not only strength but also joy while embracing these newfound qualities without hesitation or fearfully clinging to what once held her back before embarking on this journey. In fact, letting go of those fears entirely allowed Linda to discover who she was really meant to become—someone greater than who she started out as!

Linda's journey is a beautiful illustration of the quote from late spiritual leader Sri Chinmoy:

"If we fearfully cling

To what we have,

We will never be able to discover

Who we really are."

The principle of nonattachment is often misunderstood as a practice of detaching oneself from the world. In reality, the core meaning of nonattachment is to detach oneself from the idea that the world defines *who we are*. People define their own world, and in order to do so, they need to begin with understanding themselves. This can be achieved through practices such as nonattachment meditation or yoga, or even by simply taking time throughout the day to observe where external factors are influencing one's definition of self. As people consciously release these external labels, their inner barriers will begin to dissipate and their true self will have the opportunity to shine through and flourish. It is through this practice of nonattachment that people can truly discover and embrace their authentic selves.

The concept of nonattachment is prevalent in many spiritual traditions, with the idea that attachment to things can lead to suffering. In Buddhism, this is one of the Four Noble Truths, highlighting the importance of letting go of one's attachments. Similarly, Aparigraha is one of the fundamental ethical rules in yoga, emphasizing the need to practice non-greed and nonattachment. Even the Gospel of Luke in Christianity has teachings on not being attached to material possessions. While it may seem counterintuitive to not hold on to things people value, perhaps true freedom is found in releasing oneself from the things that weigh one down.

Acceptance and commitment therapy (ACT) is a therapeutic approach that emphasizes psychological flexibility. In ACT, attachment is a key concept that is closely tied to the ability to observe one's thoughts, feelings, and beliefs. This allows for a more flexible response to the present moment, rather than rigidly following the mind's rules, old schemas, or shoulds.

ACT distinguishes between "self-as-content" and "self-as-context" to clarify the difference in perspective. When an individual is attached to self-as-content, they may believe that the stories their mind tells them about themselves are true and may not see the bigger picture. For example, someone might believe that they are *good at math and bad at writing* or that they are a *good mother*. However, this attachment to one's ego can be problematic when things don't go as expected or when change occurs. Being stuck in self-satisfaction may prevent someone from paying attention to important feedback that could help them grow.

On the other hand, self-as-context is a way of looking at oneself that allows for more flexibility and options. Rather than being attached to the ego, self-as-context acknowledges that an individual is constantly changing. They may be *good at math and bad at writing* at one time, and the opposite at another time. They may be a *good mother* in some situations but not in others. Self-as-context encourages individuals to see themselves with an open mind, from different perspectives, and to understand that their sense of self is not fixed. This perspective can help individuals find a deeper sense of who they are beyond material things, life roles, and time. It enables them to connect with the world around them and embrace their uniqueness.

How to Cultivate Nonattachment with Self-As-Context

Normal is overrated. People are constantly bombarded by societal standards that tell them how they should look, think, and behave. But what if we were to tell you that these expectations are entirely made up? According to Steven Hayes, there is no universal definition of "normal" when it comes to mental health or intelligence. Rather, each individual brings their own unique set of skills and strengths to the table. So instead of comparing oneself to some imaginary "normal" person, why not focus on one's individual progress? Whether it's developing a new hobby or improving relationships, the important thing is to measure oneself against one's own personal benchmarks. As writer Joseph Ciarrchi says, *let's find a way to "do our life, our way" and embrace the wonderful quirks that make us who we are. After all, normal is just a setting on the washing machine.*

In order to cultivate nonattachment and reduce attachment to ego, individuals can adopt a **practice of "sometimes" thinking**. The idea is to recognize when the mind is creating inflexible self-stories such as "I am" or "I can't," and instead add the disclaimer "sometimes" to such thoughts. This creates space and helps one to recognize the impermanence of the self. For example, someone who believes "I am anxious" can shift to "I am anxious sometimes." This practice can help people see themselves as more than the story their mind creates and be open to exploring options and taking risks.

Imagine Helen, who has struggled with anxiety for a long time. She tends to think of herself as "an anxious person," and this self-labeling *reinforces her belief that she is powerless to change her anxious tendencies.* One day, she decides to try the "sometimes" thinking practice to see if it helps her shift her mindset.

When Helen notices herself thinking "I am anxious," she adds the disclaimer "sometimes" to the end of the thought. She tells herself, "I am anxious sometimes," and takes a deep breath. She begins to realize that her anxiety is not a fixed trait, but rather a passing emotion that comes and goes. She is more than just her anxiety, and she has the ability to take steps to manage it when it arises.

As Helen continues to practice "sometimes" thinking, she notices that she is less attached to her anxious thoughts and feelings. She begins to see herself as a dynamic, multifaceted individual, rather than a fixed entity defined by her anxiety. This newfound sense of openness allows her to explore new possibilities and take risks she might not have considered before. By adopting this practice, Sarah has cultivated a greater sense of nonattachment and reduced her attachment to her ego, leading to a more fulfilling and empowered life.

The idea of **seeing oneself as interdependent** is an important concept that is often overlooked in society's emphasis on individualism. Despite the myth of self-reliance, humans are highly social creatures who require connection and interaction with others in order to survive. By recognizing this interdependence, individuals can begin to see how their well-being is intertwined with the well-being of others.

In competitive environments such as academia, it may be tempting to view others as opponents to be defeated in order to achieve success. However, research has shown that choosing cooperation over competition can lead to better outcomes for all involved. Instead of competing with friends, co-workers, or siblings, individuals can try collaborating with them to achieve mutual success. By adopting a win-win mindset rather than a win-lose one, people can foster positive relationships and achieve more than they would through competition.

In addition to improving individual outcomes, seeing oneself as interdependent can also lead to more positive societal outcomes. By recognizing our reliance on others, people may be more likely to prioritize community well-being and social justice. Overall, embracing the idea of interdependence can lead to a more holistic and fulfilling life, as well as a more cooperative and equitable society.

Expanding on the concept of interdependence, let's connect it to Helen's example of dealing with criticism from her inner critic and her resounding belief that *she is powerless to change her anxious tendencies*. When Helen recognizes that her self-criticisms stem from a deep-rooted need for validation and approval from others, she can begin to see how her well-being is interconnected with the well-being of others. By understanding that she is not an isolated individual, but rather a part of a larger social fabric, she can start to shift her mindset from a self-focused one to another-focused one.

In practice, this means that instead of viewing her self-criticisms as a personal flaw, Helen can recognize that her negative self-talk stems from societal pressures to conform to certain standards. By acknowledging this, she can then take steps to overcome her self-criticisms by seeking support and guidance from her community. For instance, she could reach out to a trusted friend or family member and ask for their feedback on her work or behavior, instead of relying solely on her own self-judgment. This collaborative approach not only helps Helen achieve her goals but also strengthens her relationships with others, fostering a sense of mutual support and interdependence.

Practicing nonattachment can be challenging, and fostering interdependence can trigger defensiveness, especially if one has been hyper-independent all their life. Therefore, **one important aspect of nonattachment is being open to feedback.** Often, individuals have rigid beliefs about themselves and are resistant to others' ideas. However, this can hinder growth and adaptation over time. Therefore, being open to feedback is crucial for personal and professional development.

For example, imagine a team leader who has a tendency to micromanage their team. They may believe that this is the best way to ensure the quality of the work, but in reality, this behavior can be counterproductive and demotivating for team members. By being open to feedback and considering different perspectives, the leader can recognize the negative impact of their actions and adapt their behavior to be more collaborative and empowering for the team.

Continuing with Helen's example, if she wants to improve her interdependence and reduce her attachment to ego, she may need to be open to feedback from others. For instance, if Helen is working on a project with a colleague and receives feedback that her ideas are not aligning with the group's goals, she may become defensive and refuse to adapt. However, if she practices nonattachment and recognizes that her self-worth is not tied to her ideas, she may be more open to receiving feedback and making necessary adjustments to achieve the best outcome for the group. By being receptive to feedback, Sarah can improve her relationships and her work performance while also reducing her attachment to rigid self-stories.

Expanding the example a little further, consider that Helen is a graduate student who is working on her thesis. She's been struggling with writing and often feels anxious about her progress. She's also noticed that her relationships with her friends and family have been strained because of her stress levels.

In order to reduce her attachment to her ego and the idea that she must succeed on her own, Helen decides to adopt a collaborative mindset. She reaches out to other graduate students in her program and suggests forming a writing group. Together, they can share their work, provide feedback, and support each other through the writing process.

At first, Helen is hesitant to share her work and receive feedback. However, as she begins to hear other students' perspectives and suggestions, she realizes that their feedback is valuable and helps her improve her writing. She also notices that the writing group has helped her feel less isolated and more connected to her peers.

By adopting a collaborative mindset and being open to feedback, Helen is able to reduce her attachment to her ego and the idea that she must succeed on her own. She's able to see how her well-being is intertwined with the well-being of others and how cooperation can lead to better outcomes for everyone involved. Through the writing group, she's able to make progress on her thesis and improve her relationships with those around her.

Overall, practicing nonattachment involves letting go of attachment to being right, being open to feedback, recognizing one's interdependence, and adopting a "sometimes" mindset. By taking actionable steps toward nonattachment, individuals can lead more fulfilling and adaptive lives.

Being interdependent will ultimately help people hold multiple perspectives. One can start by consciously seeking out diverse viewpoints. For instance, when encountering a challenging situation or issue, instead of only considering one's own perspective, one can actively seek out the views of others involved (Sarah and her writing group). By seeking out diverse viewpoints, individuals can expand their own perspectives and cultivate a sense of interdependence. This can help break down the rigid beliefs that can come with attachment to ego, and encourage a more open and flexible approach to life. For example, if Sarah is working on a writing project and is feeling stuck, she can reach out to her writing group for feedback and different perspectives.

By being open to their ideas and suggestions, she may be able to see the project in a new light and find new solutions to any issues she is facing. This could involve having a conversation with a colleague, listening to a friend's perspective, or even seeking out the opinions of people who hold different beliefs or values.

Consider this: Sarah is a manager at a marketing firm, and she has been tasked with coming up with a new advertising campaign for a client. In the past, she has always relied on her own creative ideas and intuition to come up with successful campaigns. However, she has been learning about the importance of interdependence and nonattachment, and she wants to try a new approach.

Instead of relying solely on her own ideas, Sarah decides to seek out diverse viewpoints from her team members. She sets up a brainstorming session and encourages everyone to contribute their ideas and perspectives. During the session, she makes an effort to listen actively to each team member and not dismiss any ideas outright. She also encourages her team members to build on each other's ideas and collaborate to create the most effective campaign.

By being open to diverse viewpoints and fostering collaboration, Sarah and her team are able to create a campaign that is not only successful but also inclusive and reflective of diverse perspectives. Moreover, the process of seeking out diverse viewpoints and collaborating with her team has helped Sarah see the benefits of interdependence and nonattachment. She now understands that she doesn't need to rely solely on her own ideas or hold rigid beliefs about her abilities in order to be successful. By recognizing the interdependence between herself and her team, Sarah has become a more effective and adaptable leader.

Putting oneself in someone else's shoes and considering their experience and perspective is paramount. For instance, if one is having a disagreement with a coworker, instead of immediately assuming they are wrong, one could try to understand their perspective and see the situation from their point of view. Engaging in activities that promote diverse perspectives, such as reading books from different cultures or attending cultural events, can also help expand one's awareness and broaden their perspectives.

An example of holding multiple perspectives could be when dealing with a difficult family situation. Instead of only considering one's own needs and wants, one could try to understand the perspectives of other family members involved. This might involve having a conversation with them and actively listening to their point of view. By doing so, one could gain a better understanding of the situation and work toward a resolution that takes everyone's needs and perspectives into account.

Another example could be in the workplace, when working on a team project. Instead of only considering one's own ideas and solutions, one could actively seek out the viewpoints of other team members. This could involve having brainstorming sessions or encouraging open dialogue to allow for multiple perspectives to be shared. By doing so, the team can work toward a more well-rounded and effective solution that takes into account the various perspectives and ideas of all team members.

To practice nonattachment and hold multiple perspectives, it can be helpful to ask oneself **reflective questions.** For example, *one can ask what stories they tell themselves that stop them from moving forward, what roles they hold in their family or workplace that may be limiting them, and what would become possible if they let go of those roles.* By challenging and expanding one's perspective in this way, they can begin to see their experience from many different angles.

Consider this scenario: You had a disagreement with a friend and the situation has been bothering you for a few days. You're struggling to let go of your anger and frustration.

Reflective Questioning:
- What specific thoughts and feelings are you experiencing about this situation?
- What underlying assumptions are you making about your friend's intentions and actions?
- What evidence do you have to support these assumptions?
- Is there any evidence to contradict them?

- Are there any personal biases or past experiences that may be influencing your perspective on this situation?
- How would you feel if you were in your friend's shoes?
- How might they be experiencing this situation?
- What is your ultimate goal in this situation?
- Is holding on to your anger and frustration helping you achieve that goal?
- Are there any alternative ways to view this situation or approach it that might be more constructive?
- What actions can you take to address this situation in a way that aligns with your values and goals, and that takes into account the perspectives and feelings of both yourself and your friend?

In addition, it is essential to learn to let go of outcomes and recognize the reality of a situation. For instance, once a work has been released into the world, there is no going back, and the outcome is out of one's control. While this can be challenging, accepting this fact can ultimately lead to a sense of calm and freedom from attachment to the outcome.

To illustrate the concept of letting go of control, one can imagine trying to mentally control the movement of a pencil. No matter how strong one's will, they cannot move the pencil without physically touching it. Similarly, trying to control outcomes in life can be futile and can lead to unnecessary stress and attachment. Instead, by embracing multiple perspectives and letting go of outcomes, one can cultivate a greater sense of openness and flexibility in their life.

CURATING YOUR MEDIA CONSUMPTION

Almost everyone knows the feeling of getting sucked into the endless vortex of bad news. It's like a black hole that draws people in, swallowing them whole. It's called doom scrolling, and it's become all too common in today's world. It's no wonder the name fits the behavior perfectly. From Covid-19 statistics to natural disasters and political upheaval, people's timelines are often filled with negative news stories. But what people may not know is that the constant consumption of negative news can have harmful effects on one's mental health. Research has shown that it can lead to increased fear, stress, anxiety, and sadness (Baumeister, 2001). So, if individuals want to protect their mental wellbeing, they need to start being mindful of what they consume, and remember that balance is key.

Conscious media consumption describes the practice of being mindful and intentional about what media people consume and how they consume it. According to Stephanie Harrison, a positive psychology researcher and founder of the New Happy, this involves paying attention to both what people consume and how they consume it. In today's world, it's easy to get caught up in mindless scrolling or binge-watching as a way to distract oneself from difficult emotions or situations. However, Harrison argues that consuming media in this way can have negative consequences on people's mental health.

By being conscious of what media they consume, people can minimize exposure to negative news or content that may trigger anxiety or stress. They can also seek out media that promotes positive messages and connects them with others. Additionally, being intentional about how they consume media can help them avoid multitasking or using it as a form of avoidance, which can lead to decreased attention span and increased feelings of restlessness. In essence, conscious media consumption means being present and intentional with one's media usage, allowing people to reap the benefits of positive media while minimizing the negative effects on their mental health.

How to Control and Curate What Is Consumed and Let Go of Negativity

To practice mindful social media use, it's important to be aware of why one is scrolling. Is one looking to connect with others and build relationships, or are they trying to fill a void or distract themselves from difficult emotions? When people use social media to stay connected with loved ones, share things that matter to them, and engage in building new relationships, it can increase their well-being and sense of connection. However, when they use social media out of fear and anxiety, such as fearing that they may miss out on something or feeling disconnected if they're not using social media, it can take a toll on their mental health and well-being.

Psychotherapist and behavior specialist Dr. Steven Rosenberg stresses the importance of finding a balance when it comes to media consumption. While people have more ways than ever to stay connected to the internet, consuming a vast amount of information from various sources requires a mindful approach. People should ensure that the media they view is entertaining and helps them learn something. By being aware of their motivations and focusing on intentional and mindful consumption, they can protect their mental health and well-being while staying connected to the world around them.

In a world where people are bombarded with content on a daily basis, it can be challenging to filter out the noise and find the type of content that truly resonates with them. However, aligning one's consumption with one's values and goals is crucial for maintaining one's overall well-being. Harrison's "Learn/Connect/Joy" rule offers a practical way to approach this process. By analyzing whether people are learning, connecting, or finding joy in the content they consume, they can make informed decisions about what to keep and what to let go. This approach not only helps them stay true to their values but also ensures that they are investing their time and energy into content that enriches their lives. So, if they find themselves feeling drained or uninspired after scrolling through their feed, perhaps it's time to reevaluate whose content one is following.

In today's digital age, the internet has become an inevitable part of our lives. From social media to online news, there's an abundance of online content available at our fingertips. However, with this convenience comes a responsibility to set our own boundaries. As Harrison rightly suggests, certain content can be harmful, but what's harmful for one person may not be harmful for another. It's essential to identify our unique circumstances and figure out what upsets or challenges us. Dr. Rosenberg highlights the importance of setting goals and finding a balance between online and real-life activities. In essence, we have to take charge of our digital lives and view only the things that will enhance our well-being.

Making small changes in how people use social media can have a big impact on their well-being. While it might seem overwhelming to navigate the endless rabbit-hole of Instagram, taking conscious viewing one step at a time can make a difference. By consciously curating one's social media feed to include positive contributors and setting limits on its usage, people can become more mindful and feel good about their choices. According to Dr. Rosenberg and Harrison, practicing mindful habits when using social media can be as simple as setting a timer or checking it only at certain times of the day. These small changes can help them take control of their social media usage and positively impact their mental health.

Practicing mindfulness is not just restricted to yoga mats or meditation sessions. It can be incorporated into daily life, even in the world of the internet. The principle of conscious consumption emphasizes intention and encourages people to take a step back before they dive into a digital world of distraction. By acknowledging one's emotions and pausing before reaching for one's phones or laptops, people give themselves a moment to check in with themselves. Just like in meditation, this pause can help people recognize their thoughts and feelings, redirect their focus, and regain control of their attention. By applying mindfulness to our online experiences, people can craft a more intentional and fulfilling life, both online and off.

In a world where social media and news platforms can be overwhelming and inundated with negative content, it's important to be mindful and intentional about curating our media consumption. Here are some realistic ways to break the chain of negativity:

Step 1: Be cautious and conscious of how much bad media you are consuming so

that you can cut out (or minimize) the toxicity.

It's crucial to be aware of the kind of media people are consuming and how it affects them. One way to do this is to monitor one's reactions to certain content. For example, if someone finds themselves feeling anxious or upset after reading the news, they may want to limit their exposure to those topics. They can also choose to unfollow or mute accounts that consistently share negative or triggering content. This can be challenging, especially if they feel that they need to stay informed about current events, but setting boundaries is essential for one's mental health.

Another way to limit one's exposure to negative media is to take a break from social media altogether. This could mean deleting apps for a certain amount of time, or simply limiting the amount of time one spends on social media each day. By doing this, people give themselves the opportunity to disconnect and focus on other activities that bring them joy and positivity.

Step 2: Introspect. Ask your inner circle for recommendations, as this will help you prioritize the media you enjoy and build positivity in your feed.

It's easy to get caught up in the endless scroll of social media, but it's important to be intentional about the kind of content one consumes. One way to do this is to reflect on one's values and priorities and seek out media that aligns with them. For example, if someone values mental health and wellness, they can follow accounts that share positive affirmations, self-care tips, and resources for managing stress and anxiety.

Another way to curate one's media consumption is to ask one's inner circle for recommendations. Friends and family members can be a great resource for finding new podcasts, books, and TV shows that bring joy and positivity. By prioritizing the media one enjoys, people can build a feed that is filled with content that aligns with their values and goals.

Step 3: Set time limits on apps to minimize your media consumption.

Setting time limits on social media apps is another way to break the chain of negativity. People can use the settings on their phones to limit the amount of time they spend on social media each day. This can help them be more mindful about the time they spend online and ensure that they are not consuming too much negative content. They can also use apps that track their screen time and give them reminders to take breaks and disconnect.

Above all, it's important to remember that progress is not linear and takes time. Curating one's media consumption is a process, and it may take time to find the right balance that works for everyone. It's okay to make mistakes and slip up, but it's important to keep trying and be intentional about the media one consumes. By taking small steps each day, people can build a feed that is filled with positivity and joy.

For example, let's say someone is trying to curate their social media feed to focus on mental health and wellness. They can start by unfollowing accounts that consistently share triggering or negative content. They can also seek out accounts that share positive affirmations, self-care tips, and resources for managing stress and anxiety. They can ask their friends and family members for recommendations for podcasts, books, and TV shows that focus on mental health and wellness. People can also set time limits on social media apps to ensure that we are not spending too much time online. For example, we can set a limit of thirty minutes per day on Instagram.

In addition to setting time limits, it's important to be mindful of when and how people use social media. For example, people can designate specific times of the day when they check their feeds, and avoid using social media while they're engaged in other activities, like work or spending time with friends and family.

In conclusion, media consumption plays a significant role in one's mental health and well-being. The chain of negativity can be broken by being cautious and conscious of the media people consume, prioritizing positivity in one's feeds, and setting time limits on apps. By taking these steps, people can build a healthier media diet and promote a more positive and fulfilling life.

Chapter Takeaways

- The notion of the inner critic is a well-known concept in psychology that pertains to the pessimistic voice that often exists within our minds. This voice evaluates, disapproves, and rebukes us for our perceived deficiencies and limitations.
- Patrick Gaudreau, a psychology professor at the University of Ottawa, introduced the concept of excellentism. It entails establishing lofty benchmarks for oneself, but not letting those standards become unrealistic or harmful to one's health. Instead of self-criticism when falling short, individuals can opt to embrace novel experiences, utilize innovative approaches to problem-solving, and learn from their errors as they persistently aim for excellence.
- Nonattachment is a technique of relinquishing the urge to manage, cling to, or possess things in life. It does not imply becoming disconnected or

apathetic, but rather accepting that everything in life is transient and in a constant state of flux. By releasing attachment, individuals can encounter greater independence and less distress.

- The expression conscious media consumption pertains to the practice of being attentive and purposeful about the media that individuals choose to consume and how they consume it. Stephanie Harrison suggests that this requires individuals to pay attention to both the content of what they consume and their manner of consumption.

Chapter 3: The Growth Mindset

There is a powerful connection between having a growth mindset and being able to let go. When people cultivate a growth mindset, they believe that their abilities and intelligence can be developed through effort and persistence, rather than being fixed traits. This perspective empowers them to see failures and setbacks as opportunities for growth and learning. By embracing a growth mindset, they are more likely to let go of limiting beliefs and self-doubt, and instead focus on their ability to learn and improve. They become less attached to their mistakes and more willing to take risks, which can lead to greater success and fulfilment in all areas of their lives. Letting go becomes easier when they trust in their own abilities and know that they can continue to grow and improve over time.

EMBRACING CHANGE

Embracing change is essential to a growth mindset because it allows individuals to view challenges and setbacks as opportunities for learning and development. Therefore, having a growth mindset is crucial when it comes to letting go. By possessing a growth mindset, individuals understand that the mere threat of failure is not an endpoint but rather a steppingstone to success. This perspective allows them to approach any given situation with a sense of curiosity and openness to learning. It allows them to let go of outdated beliefs and negative self-talk, and they are able to embrace new challenges and opportunities for growth. Whether it's forgiving oneself for past mistakes or moving on from toxic relationships, letting go requires a willingness to release the things that hold one back, and embrace the limitless possibilities of the future.

A growth mindset is the belief that one's abilities and intelligence can be developed through hard work, dedication, and perseverance. Individuals with a growth mindset see failure as a temporary setback and use it as a steppingstone to improve and grow.

Change is an inevitable part of life, and individuals who embrace it are more likely to adapt to new situations, learn new skills, and grow as individuals. Change often brings challenges, and individuals who approach those challenges with a growth mindset are more likely to learn from them and find solutions to overcome them.

For example, imagine a student who receives a poor grade on a test. A fixed mindset would view this as a reflection of their intelligence and ability, leading them to feel defeated and give up. A growth mindset, on the other hand, would view the poor grade as an opportunity to learn from their mistakes, identify areas where they need to improve, let go of the unnecessary guilt and develop a plan to do better next time.

Embracing change also allows individuals to take risks and step outside of their comfort zones. When people are open to new experiences and willing to take risks, they are more likely to discover new passions, develop new skills, and achieve their goals. In essence, embracing change is elemental to a growth mindset because it allows individuals to view challenges as opportunities for growth and development. It enables individuals to adapt to new situations, learn new skills, and take risks that lead to personal growth and achievement.

Fear of change is a common human emotion, and it can be driven by a variety of psychological factors. Zaval, Markowitz, and Weber (2015) conducted a study to investigate people's preferences for maintaining the status quo versus taking a risk and making a change. They found that individuals tend to be loss averse, meaning they are more sensitive to losses than gains. This loss aversion leads people to overvalue the costs of changing and undervalue the potential benefits. In the study, participants were presented with different scenarios and asked to make a choice. The researchers found that people were more likely to take risks when the choice was framed as a loss, rather than a gain. This suggests that people are more motivated by the fear of losing something they already have than by the potential benefits of change. Overall, the study highlights the importance of understanding the psychological factors that underlie people's fear of change and refusing to let go of what is familiar.

Another reason people may be afraid of change is because it can disrupt their sense of control and stability. In a study by Lerner and colleagues (2015), participants who were given the opportunity to choose their own music were more willing to take risks in a gambling task than those who had no control over the music. The study suggested that when people feel like they have control over a situation, they are more willing to take risks and embrace change.

Moreover, people may be afraid of change because it requires effort and discomfort. A study by Zou and colleagues (2016) found that people are less likely to engage in pro-environmental behaviors because they perceive them as inconvenient and uncomfortable. The study suggested that people need to believe that their actions will have a significant impact on the environment and that the benefits of change outweigh the costs in order to be motivated to change their behavior.

In conclusion, people may be afraid of change because of loss aversion, a desire for control and stability, and discomfort. By understanding these psychological factors, individuals and organizations can develop strategies to overcome the fear of change and embrace growth and improvement.

Change, no matter the type or scale, requires both thought and emotion. It's not just about learning the mechanics of how to ride a bike, but also about feeling confident enough to take off those training wheels. It's not just about proposing a project to spend company money, but also about the fear of rejection and the possibility of failure. And it's not just about renovating a house, but also about the attachment and memories that come with it. This emotional aspect of change is often overlooked, but it's a crucial part of the process. The change model developed by psychologists Don Kelley and Daryl Connor takes this into account, helping individuals navigate the ups and downs of change with empathy and understanding. By recognizing the emotions involved and addressing them in a healthy way, change can become less daunting and more manageable.

Change can often stir up a range of emotions that can leave people feeling like they're going off the rails. However, understanding the emotional cycle of change can help bring a sense of normalcy to this rollercoaster of feelings. This cycle is present in various scenarios, such as adjusting to new leadership or board structure and when acquiring new competencies. By acknowledging the different stages of change, including denial, resistance, exploration, commitment, and acknowledgement, people can gain a better understanding of the emotions they face and come out on the other side better equipped to handle them. It's important to remember that change is a process, and with the right mindset, it can lead to growth and transformation for both individuals and organizations.

The emotional cycle of change is composed of five stages: uninformed optimism, informed pessimism, valley of despair, informed optimism, and success and fulfilment. The first stage, uninformed optimism, is marked by excitement and anticipation of the benefits that change will bring, but without acknowledging the costs. The second stage, informed pessimism, sets in as people begin to realize the reality of the effort required for change, leading to negative emotions and doubt. The third stage is the lowest point, the valley of despair, where many people give up due to the discomfort and distance of the perceived benefits. If people persevere through this stage, they will reach the fourth stage of informed optimism, where the possibility of success increases and the benefits of change become more apparent. Finally, the fifth stage, success and fulfilment, is reached when the new behaviors become routine, the benefits are fully experienced, and the cost of change is perceived as worth it.

The key to overcoming the emotional cycle of change is to have a compelling future vision of what an individual wants to achieve, and to persevere through the difficult times.

Here's an example to help illustrate the five stages of change:

Say, someone decides to start going to the gym to get in better shape.

Uninformed optimism: In this stage, the person is excited about the idea of going to the gym. They imagine the benefits of being in shape—having more energy, feeling more confident, etc.—but haven't actually experienced any of the downsides yet, such as the time and effort it takes to get to the gym regularly.

Informed pessimism: After a few trips to the gym, the person may start to feel discouraged. They may realize how difficult it is to stick to a routine, how sore their muscles can get, and how busy the gym can be at certain times. They may question whether it's really worth the effort to keep going.

Valley of despair: At this point, the person may hit a low point and consider giving up. Maybe they've missed a few days at the gym, and the idea of starting over feels daunting. They may feel like they're not seeing any results and wonder if all the effort is even worth it. This is a critical stage because if they quit here, they'll have to start all over again.

Informed optimism: If they can push through the valley of despair, they may start to see progress. They may notice that they can lift heavier weights or run for longer distances than when they started. This progress can be motivating, and they may feel more optimistic about reaching their goal.

Success and fulfilment: Finally, after several weeks or months of consistent effort, the person may start to experience the benefits of their hard work. They may feel more confident, have more energy, and notice changes in their body shape. At this point, going to the gym may feel like a normal, routine part of their life, and the initial struggles may feel like a distant memory.

Ways to Overcome the Fear of Change

Tackling Underlying Fears

If one's fear of change is based on underlying fears like fear of failure or fear of criticism, they can overcome them by changing their beliefs about failure and criticism. For example, if an individual fears failure, they need to understand that it's a natural part of the learning process and everyone experiences it at some point. By changing their mindset about failure, and understanding that it's not a reflection of their worth as a person, they can be more resilient and persistent in the face of obstacles. Similarly, if one fears criticism, they need to examine whether the opinions of others are really worth conforming to. By understanding that one has the power to shape their own life and make their own choices, they can overcome the fear of criticism and pursue the changes that are important to them.

For example, imagine a person wants to start a new business, but they fear failure. By changing their mindset and reframing failure as an opportunity to learn and grow, they can approach the challenge with a more positive attitude. They can also seek out the advice and support of others who have been through similar experiences, which can help them build their confidence and overcome their fear of failure.

Consider Jasper's struggle: He was struggling with a difficult decision. He had always dreamed of running his own small business but couldn't shake the fear of failing. He was convinced that if he tried, he would only end up making mistakes and ultimately wasting time and money. It wasn't until he talked to a friend who had started their own successful business that he began to see things differently. By reframing failure as an opportunity to learn and grow, Jasper was able to change his mindset and approach his dream with a more positive attitude. Seeking out the advice and support of others who had been through similar experiences also helped him build his confidence and overcome his fear of failure.

Now, Jasper is on his way to fulfilling his dream and is grateful for the mindset shift that got him there.

Re-framing Change

If one has had negative experiences with change in the past, they can overcome their fear of change by embracing it more often. By exposing themselves to new experiences and challenges, they can build resilience and adaptability. They can also reframe change as an opportunity for growth and learning, rather than something to be feared or avoided.

For example, if someone has a fear of public speaking, they can start by taking small steps like speaking in front of a small group of friends or family members. As they build their confidence, they can gradually work their way up to larger audiences or more high-pressure situations. By reframing public speaking as an opportunity to share their knowledge and connect with others, they can overcome their fear and pursue new opportunities.

Overcoming Natural Human Weakness

Humans are wired to seek instant gratification and avoid pain, which can make it difficult to pursue long-term goals or make lasting changes in one's life. However, by leveraging these tendencies in a positive way, individuals can overcome their natural weaknesses and achieve their goals. For example, if someone wants to lose weight, they can break down the goal into smaller, more manageable steps, like eating a healthy breakfast each day or going for a short walk after dinner. By focusing on these small wins and celebrating their progress along the way, they can stay motivated and overcome the natural tendency to give up or lose sight of their goals. They can also find ways to make the process more enjoyable or rewarding, such as listening to their favorite music while they exercise or rewarding themselves with a small treat after reaching a milestone.

BRAIN DUMPING

Life is filled with countless thoughts running through one's mind every minute of every day. Some are essential to one's survival, while others are trivial and unnecessary. But when these thoughts become overwhelming, it can feel like the mind is cluttered and chaotic. This is what experts call *mental clutter*. It is the accumulation of negative self-talk, worries, doubts, and fears that hinder people from focusing on what really matters. Just like physical clutter, mental clutter can affect one's mental health, creativity, and productivity. It's important to acknowledge mental clutter and find ways to clear the mind so that people can function at their best.

Mental clutter can take many different forms, such as obsessive thoughts or negative self-talk. It can also manifest as excessive planning or an inability to focus on the present moment. Perfectionism and a constant need for control are also common culprits of mental clutter. Perhaps one finds themselves replaying past mistakes over and over again, or constantly worrying about a future event that may not even happen. All of these are examples of mental clutter, and they can have a profound impact on one's emotions, decisions, and overall well-being. Ultimately making it incredibly hard for people to let go and move on.

Brain dumping, a tool popularized by productivity consultant David Allen, is a technique to help organize one's thoughts and close any lingering "open loops" in one's mind. However, putting this technique into practice may not always be as easy as it sounds. Sometimes, when people are feeling anxious or are under a lot of stress, thoughts race too fast to follow, let alone put down on paper. It can be a daunting task to try to make sense of the chaos in one's mind. Nevertheless, all individuals want to let go of the overwhelming thoughts that clutter their heads. Despite the challenges, with practice, anyone can master the art of brain dumping and reap the benefits of a clearer mind.

A brain dump can be compared to emptying out one's backpack at the end of a long day. Just like how students unload all their notebooks, pencils, and textbooks onto their desk, a brain dump involves getting everything out of one's head and onto paper or a screen. It can feel overwhelming at first, much like a chaotic pile of school supplies on one's desk, but once the individual starts organizing and processing the information, they feel much more relaxed and able to tackle their tasks with a clear mind. So, think of a brain dump as a necessary process, just like organizing one's backpack to start fresh each day.

By creating space, people may find that their newfound open-mindedness leads to a surge of creativity. If individuals are wondering why they should start doing a brain dump, there are plenty of reasons to consider. However, the biggest benefit of a brain dump is that it allows people to clear their mind of unnecessary worries and tasks. When someone has a lot on their plate, everything can feel urgent and important, which can leave them feeling overwhelmed and stressed. By taking the time to write down everything that's on their mind, they'll gain a better perspective on what's truly important and what can wait.

Additionally, a brain dump helps people to set aside the "shoulds" in one's life—those things that they feel pressured to do but never seem to accomplish. With a clear list of priorities, they can focus on what really matters and can achieve a greater sense of productivity and peace of mind. Similar to how clutter can make one's home feel overwhelming, mental clutter can make their minds feel like they're in overdrive. Their thoughts throughout the day can be difficult to concentrate on, and some of them can cause mental clutter.

Mental clutter can take many forms, such as information overload, which is when people have too much information to process and it leads to feeling mentally drained. Studies have shown that information overload negatively impacts our ability to focus, make decisions, and retain information. It can also lead to anxiety and burnout, affecting our overall well-being. Therefore, it is important to be mindful of our exposure to information and take breaks to recharge our mental batteries (Cheng & Wenhua, 2022). Expectations are another form of mental clutter, where individuals want things or people to be a certain way, but they just don't happen. Tasks that they're procrastinating on can also contribute to mental clutter, constantly nagging at the back of their minds throughout the day. Finally, negative feelings like stress, anxiety, worry, fear, shame, anger, and frustration can all create mental clutter.

If people don't filter out the noise in their thoughts, they can become easily irritated throughout the day, making it difficult to focus and be productive. Their minds can jump between different thoughts and distractions, from current events to mundane tasks to celebrity gossip, leading to even more mental clutter. To help them incorporate this beneficial practice into their life and gain more control, relaxation, and confidence, it's time to explore some tips for brain dumping.

Try a Simple Brain Dump Exercise

The brain dump exercise is a simple and effective way to clear one's mind and get organized. This exercise allows people to put all their thoughts and ideas down on paper so they can free up space in their mind and focus on what's important. **To get started, grab a sheet of paper or open a computer file** and write a sentence that will guide your thoughts. For example, individuals can write, "*What should I be aware of right now?*" "*What task should I focus on right now?*" "*What are the benefits of . . .?*" or "*What dangers are there in . . .?*" The sentence they choose will depend on what they want to achieve from the exercise.

Once they have written their sentence, they need to set a timer for ten minutes. During this time, they allow themselves to write down everything that comes to mind, without editing or filtering their thoughts. If they get stuck or can't think of anything to write, they just repeat the sentence that was written at the beginning and continue writing.

The goal of this exercise is to get everything out of one's head and onto paper. This can include anything from one's to-do list, ideas, worries, and even dreams. By doing this exercise regularly, people can train their mind to be more focused and less cluttered with thoughts that don't serve them.

For example, let's say one is feeling overwhelmed with all the tasks they need to complete for work. They decide to do a brain dump exercise using the sentence: *What task should I focus on right now?* Then, they set a timer for ten minutes and start writing down all the tasks that come to mind. They write down everything from small tasks, like sending an email, to big projects, like completing a report. After ten minutes, they review their list and prioritize the tasks based on urgency and importance. They can now focus on completing the most important tasks first, knowing that they have everything written down and organized.

Now that they have their brain dumps on paper, what exactly are they supposed to do with them? Keeping one's brain dumps and reviewing them is crucial to getting the most out of the process. Not only does it help people track their progress and ideas, but it can also serve as a source of inspiration for future projects. One way to keep brain dumps is to use a dedicated notebook or journal. This allows individuals to keep all their ideas and thoughts in one place, making it easy to reference them later. When choosing a notebook, consider factors such as paper quality, size, and portability. For example, if someone prefers to use a fountain pen, they may want to choose a notebook with high-quality paper that won't bleed or smudge. If they need to carry their notebook with them, they should look for one that is easy to use and has a strong cover to protect it from wear and tear.

Once one has their notebook, they need to be sure to review their brain dumps regularly. They set aside time each week or month to go back through their notes and look for any ideas or insights that may have slipped their mind. This can also be a great opportunity to organize one's thoughts and ideas and identify any patterns or themes that emerge.

For example, let's say an individual is working on a new marketing campaign for their business. During a brain dump session, they jot down a bunch of ideas for social media posts, blog articles, and email newsletters. A few weeks later, they review their notes and notice that many of their ideas revolve around a particular theme or topic. This insight could help them refine their campaign strategy and create more targeted content for their audience.

Overall, keeping and reviewing one's brain dumps is a simple yet powerful way to harness the full potential of one's ideas and thoughts. With a little bit of time and effort, they can turn their brain dumps into a valuable resource that helps them stay organized, creative, and productive.

From Brain Dump to Action Items

Now that the dump is out on paper and initially reviewed, it has to be thoroughly reviewed once again to identify the actionable items. This means looking through the list of ideas, thoughts, and tasks one has written down and identifying the items that can be turned into concrete actions.

It's important to be selective and focus on the most important actions. People shouldn't try to tackle everything at once or they'll risk feeling overwhelmed and giving up before they even start. Instead, try to prioritize the items and choose the ones that are most urgent or will have the biggest impact on one's life.

Once individuals have identified their actionable items, it's time to take action on them. This can mean anything from scheduling a meeting or phone call to completing a task or project. The key is to take action immediately, rather than letting the items sit on one's list and pile up. If one finds that their brain dump is filled with too many actionable items, they need to try to limit themselves to the most important three. This will help them in avoiding feeling overwhelmed and allow them to focus on the tasks that will have the biggest impact on their life.

For example, an individual partakes in a brain dump about their work, and it includes tasks like "prepare for the upcoming meeting," "follow up with the client," and "complete the project report." Instead of trying to do all three tasks at once, they focus on the most urgent task, such as "prepare for the upcoming meeting." They set a deadline for completing this task and take action immediately, such as blocking out time on their calendar to prepare for the meeting. Once that task has been completed, they can move on to the next one.

Chapter Takeaways

- The adoption of change is vital to a growth mindset because it enables individuals to consider challenges and setbacks as occasions for learning and advancement. A growth mindset is a conviction that one's skills and intellect can be enhanced through persistent effort, devotion, and determination. People who embrace a growth mindset regard failure as a momentary obstacle and utilize it as a platform for progress and advancement.

- Altering one's perspective on failure to perceive it as a learning prospect is essential to releasing apprehension regarding change. By regarding failure as an invaluable occurrence, individuals can assimilate lessons from their errors and modify their approach to boost their prospects of success in the future. This helps them steer clear of reiterating the same mistakes or getting trapped in similar circumstances.

- Brain dumping, a tool popularized by David Allen, is a technique to help organize one's thoughts and close any lingering "open loops" in one's mind.

- Brain dumps allow people to clear their mind of unnecessary worries and tasks. When someone has a lot on their plate, everything can feel urgent and important, which can leave them feeling overwhelmed and stressed. By taking the time to write down everything that's on one's mind, they'll gain a better perspective on what's truly important and what can wait.

Chapter 4: Psychological Strategies for Letting Go

Letting go of negative self-scripts is a difficult task, but it's essential to one's mental health and well-being. One approach that has proven to be successful is externalization, also known as narrative therapy. This technique involves separating oneself from one's negative thoughts and beliefs and seeing them as an external entity that they have the power to control.

Externalization will allow readers to distance themselves from their problems by personifying their issues and viewing them from an objective point of view, promoting self-awareness and a healthier perspective. By incorporating these techniques, readers will be able to gain greater insight into themselves, their thoughts, and their behaviors, ultimately leading to a more positive and fulfilling life.

Through this strategy, people can begin to rewrite their own narrative and let go of harmful self-talk. This process may be challenging, but with the help of a therapist or self-reflection, people can begin to shift their mindset and cultivate a more positive self-image. The journey toward self-acceptance is ongoing, but with psychological strategies such as externalization, people can take small steps toward letting go of their negative self-scripts.

LETTING GO OF NEGATIVE SELF-SCRIPTS

People often find themselves engaging in a negative inner dialogue that seems to be on repeat. That's what Albert Ellis, the founder of rational-emotive-behavioral therapy, referred to as "stinking thinking." Negative scripts are essentially the pessimistic ways people think about themselves, others, or the world in general. These unconscious patterns play in the background of their minds, subtly influencing their perceptions and actions. They are like the soundtracks to their lives, and if not recognized and replaced with positive scripts, they can lead to self-sabotage and a downward spiral of negativity. But fear not! With awareness and practice, people can rewrite their inner dialogue, let go of the negative scripts, and cultivate a more optimistic outlook.

Beliefs hold so much power over one's life, yet so many unwittingly carry negative scripts that they've developed over time. These scripts are based on mistaken beliefs they formed during their early years, and they have a way of chipping away at their happiness and sense of self-worth. The thing is, the negative files in one's unconscious mind can be replaced by positive ones. It takes work, of course, but the payoff is huge. It's like going through a closet and getting rid of old clothes that don't fit anymore; once people clear out the old stuff, they make room for better, more empowering beliefs that help them lead a happier, more fulfilling life. So people shouldn't let those negative old scripts hold them back. People have the power to rewrite their story and create a brighter, more positive future for themselves.

Negative self-talk can keep people stuck in past pain and resentment by reinforcing negative beliefs about themselves and others. When people constantly berate themselves and ruminate on negative experiences, it can create a cycle of self-blame and shame, leading to feelings of helplessness and hopelessness. This can make it difficult to move forward and let go of past hurts.

On the other hand, letting go of negative self-talk can have numerous benefits for mental health. Studies have shown that self-compassion, or treating oneself with kindness and understanding, can lead to greater resilience, improved emotional well-being, and reduced symptoms of depression and anxiety (Neff, 2009; MacBeth & Gumley, 2012). Furthermore, letting go of negative self-talk can improve relationships with others. A study by Neff and colleagues (2017) found that self-compassion is associated with greater relationship satisfaction, better communication, and more supportive behaviors. In short, negative self-talk can keep you stuck in the past and lead to poor mental health outcomes, while letting go of negative self-talk and practicing self-compassion can improve resilience, emotional well-being, and relationships with others.

How to Rewrite Negative Self-scripts

Negative self-scripts can be detrimental to one's mental health and self-esteem. It's important to take the time to identify these negative thoughts and challenge them. Are they really true? Are they helpful? Individuals need to ask themselves these questions as they begin to rewrite their negative self-scripts. *Remember, just because you have thought something for a long time doesn't mean it's true.* It's time to take control of one's thoughts and start rewriting the internal script to something more positive and uplifting.

Step 1: Know Your Negative Script(s)

To rewrite negative self-scripts, it is essential to first identify and become aware of them. This involves paying attention to one's self-talk and the messages people tell themselves in different situations. People can also reflect on past experiences where they might have used negative self-talk and try to identify common themes or patterns.

Once they have identified their negative self-scripts, the next step is to challenge them and replace them with more positive and realistic self-talk. This process involves questioning the validity of one's negative beliefs and replacing them with more empowering and affirming beliefs. For instance, instead of saying "I'm going to fail. I know it," one could say "I may face some challenges, but I can overcome them and succeed if I try my best."

Studies have shown that rewriting negative self-scripts can have significant benefits for mental health and well-being. One study found that a cognitive-behavioral intervention that aimed to challenge negative self-talk and replace it with more positive self-talk was effective in reducing symptoms of depression and anxiety (McEvoy et al., 2016). Another study found that self-affirmation, or the process of replacing negative self-scripts with positive and affirming beliefs, was associated with increased resilience and decreased stress levels (Creswell et al., 2013).

In summary, to rewrite negative self-scripts, it is important to first identify and become aware of them. Then, people can challenge their validity and replace them with more positive and realistic self-talk. Consider this example: An individual has a negative script that goes like this: "I'm not good enough." This belief is triggered when the individual makes a mistake or receives criticism from others. Their negative self-talk reinforces this belief, and they start to doubt their abilities and worth.

For instance, imagine that a person has been working on a project for weeks and they receive feedback from their boss that is not entirely positive. They start to doubt their abilities, and their negative self-talk starts to take over: "I knew it. I'm not good enough for this job. I should have done better. I always mess things up."

If the individual is not aware of this negative script, it can start to shape their behavior and limit their potential. They may start to avoid taking risks, shy away from challenges, and miss out on opportunities to learn and grow. However, if they become aware of this negative script, they can start to rewrite it into something more positive and empowering. They can challenge this belief by acknowledging their strengths and accomplishments and focusing on what they can do to improve their performance. For example, they can say to themselves: "I may have made some mistakes, but I am capable of learning from them and improving. I am good enough, and I will continue to work hard and do my best."

By knowing one's negative script(s) and rewriting them, people can change the way they think and feel about themselves, and ultimately, change their behavior and achieve their goals.

Step 2: Identify the Mistaken Belief

Identifying the mistaken belief is an important step in rewriting negative self-scripts because it helps to uncover the underlying assumptions and attitudes that contribute to negative thinking patterns. Mistaken beliefs are often deeply ingrained in one's unconscious mind and can be difficult to recognize without some introspection.

From the previous example, "I knew it. I'm not good enough for this job. I should have done better. I always mess things up," the mistaken belief is "worthlessness" or "I am worthless." For example, let's say someone experiences rejection from a romantic partner and begins to think "I am unlovable." This negative self-script is based on a mistaken belief that their worth as a person is solely determined by external validation from others. The underlying basic need here might be for love and connection.

In another instance, a friend cancels an event, which might result in a negative script such as: "They don't like me and don't want to spend time with me," and the mistaken belief: "I am not worthy of love and friendship," with the individual's basic need being: *Attachment/Belonging* or *Love/Connection*.

To identify the mistaken belief, the individual would need to examine the underlying assumptions and attitudes that contribute to this negative self-script. They might ask themselves questions like "What evidence do I have that I am unlovable?" or "What would it mean if I were lovable even if this person didn't love me back?" Through this process of questioning, they might realize that the belief that they are unlovable is based on faulty reasoning or a skewed perspective.

Once the mistaken belief has been identified, the individual can begin to challenge it and reframe their thinking in a more positive and realistic way. For example, they might recognize that their worth as a person is not determined by external validation and that there are many different ways to experience love and connection.

Step 3: Tag the Unmet Basic Need

All humans have basic needs that must be met in order to thrive. From the most fundamental physiological requirements to the more complex emotional and psychological needs, each one is essential to our overall well-being. Abraham Maslow recognized this when he created his hierarchy of needs model. Abraham Maslow, the famous psychologist, identified these essential needs in his hierarchy of needs model. At the base of the pyramid is one's physiological needs, which includes things like food, water, and sleep. Without fulfilling these basic requirements, humans cannot survive.

The next level of needs is safety, which involves feeling secure and protected. This may include having a roof over one's head or being surrounded by loved ones. From there, individuals move up to love and belonging, esteem, and finally, self-actualization, which is about fulfilling one's potential and achieving one's dreams. Maslow's hierarchy reminds people of the importance of taking care of their most basic needs before pursuing higher goals.

It's easy to take these needs for granted when they are being met, but when they go unmet, the impact can be devastating. So people must take a moment to reflect on the unmet basic needs in themselves and others around them. By recognizing and addressing these needs, people can create a world where everyone has the opportunity to flourish. *Tagging the unmet basic need involves identifying the basic need that was not met during the event that triggered the negative script.* This need may be related to safety, belonging, esteem, or other basic human needs. For example, if a child grows up in an environment where they feel constantly criticized and not good enough, they may develop a negative script that says "I'm not good enough." This script may be triggered later in life when the person experiences a failure or setback.

Here's an example to illustrate how tagging the unmet basic need works:

- **Event:** A person is rejected by a romantic partner.
- **Negative Script:** "I'm unlovable."
- **Mistaken Belief:** "There is something wrong with me."
- **Tagged Unmet Basic Need:** Love and belonging.

In this example, the person's negative script is "I'm unlovable," which is based on the mistaken belief that there is something wrong with them. By tagging the unmet basic need, we can see that the person's basic need for love and belonging was not met when they were rejected by their romantic partner. This experience triggered the mistaken belief that there is something wrong with them, which led to the negative script "I'm unlovable."

By identifying the unmet basic need, the person can begin to understand why they are experiencing negative thoughts and emotions. They can also work on finding ways to meet their need for love and belonging in healthy ways, such as building positive relationships with friends and family, joining social groups, or seeking therapy.

Step 4: Rewrite the Negative Script into a Positive Script

It's common to have mistaken beliefs about oneself, others, or the world. The good news is that people can learn to rewrite these negative scripts into positive ones.

Remember, the first step is always recognizing one's negative script and identifying the mistaken belief that's fueling it. Then, tag the unmet need that's at the root of it all. By doing this, people will be able to see things from a new perspective and shift their thinking in a positive direction. With practice, they'll be able to catch those negative thoughts as they arise and replace them with more empowering ones. So go ahead and try it out—see how a positive script can transform one's mindset and life.

Rewriting a negative script into a positive script is an important step toward changing one's way of thinking and improving one's mental health. The below mentioned example will recap the concept for this final step—rewriting the negative script into a positive one.

The first step is to identify one's negative script. Negative scripts are patterns of thinking that emerge from a negative event or experience. For example, if an individual was passed over for a job promotion, their negative script might be "Why should I bother trying? Nothing good ever comes my way." It's important to be aware of one's negative scripts so that people can start to challenge and change them.

The second step is to identify the mistaken belief that underlies your negative script. Mistaken beliefs are unconscious assumptions that people hold about themselves, others, and the world around them. In the example above, the mistaken belief might be "Nothing good ever comes my way." This belief is likely rooted in past experiences where one's basic needs were not met, such as a lack of esteem or belonging.

The third step is to tag the unmet need that led to the mistaken belief. In the example above, the unmet need might be a sense of belonging or esteem, which was not fulfilled due to not receiving the job promotion. Once the individual has identified their negative script, mistaken belief, and unmet need, they can begin to rewrite the script into a more positive and realistic one. For example, the negative script "Why should I bother trying? Nothing good ever comes my way" could be rewritten as "I didn't get the promotion this time, but I will keep working hard and opportunities will come my way." This new script acknowledges the disappointment of not getting the promotion but also offers hope and motivation for the future.

Rewriting negative scripts takes time and practice, but it is a powerful tool for improving one's mental health and overall well-being. By challenging mistaken beliefs and addressing unmet needs, people can shift their thinking toward more positive and productive patterns.

Here are some more examples:

- **Know Negative Script:** I'm always so stupid.
- **Identify Mistaken Belief:** I'm not smart enough.
- **Tag Unmet Basic Need:** Esteem—self-worth.
- **Rewrite into Positive Script:** I am intelligent and capable. I just need to work harder and believe in myself.

- **Know Negative Script:** I can't do this. I'll never be good enough.

- **Identify Mistaken Belief:** I'm a failure.
- **Tag Unmet Basic Need:** Esteem—self-efficacy.
- **Rewrite into Positive Script:** This is a challenge, but I can learn and grow from it. I am capable of achieving my goals with persistence and effort.

- **Know Negative Script:** I'm always so alone.
- **Identify Mistaken Belief:** I'm unlovable.
- **Tag Unmet Basic Need:** Belonging.
- **Rewrite into Positive Script:** I have people who care about me and support me. I can strengthen my relationships and connect with others to feel more fulfilled and connected.

EXTERNALIZATION (NARRATIVE THERAPY)

Externalization therapy is a unique form of therapy that focuses on helping individuals detach themselves from the anxiety resulting from their painful memories, allowing them to let go of their past experiences. Unlike other traditional therapies, externalization therapy encourages people to view their trauma as an external entity, rather than an intrinsic part of themselves.

By separating themselves from their painful memories and experiences, individuals can gain a new perspective on their struggles and move toward a more positive and healthier life. This form of therapy can be incredibly transformative for those who are struggling to cope with traumatic experiences and can help them not only overcome their past but empower them to create a brighter future.

Externalization is also an effective method that psychologists use to help their patients deal with their problems. It can be difficult to gain perspective when people are consumed by their problems, but externalization enables them to view their symptoms or issues from an outside point of view. Drawing is one technique that psychologists use to facilitate externalization. By putting a problem "outside," people can scrutinize it without personal bias and gain insights into its true meaning or how to solve it. With this technique, patients can break free from the cycle of negative thinking and find solutions to their issues more quickly and effectively.

When people come to therapy, they often have problems that have been weighing them down for quite some time. These internal issues have yet to be fully understood and often manifest as symptoms such as anxiety, stress, or relationship problems. Externalization allows them to observe and analyze these issues from an outside perspective, patients can gain new insight and understanding into their problems. This approach can lead to faster and more effective solutions, allowing patients to find peace and resolution in their lives.

But how does externalization work, exactly? Anxiety can be all-consuming, making it easy to feel trapped by it. The more someone identifies as an anxious person, the more their condition can become impossible to escape. But what if there were a way to cope with anxiety that didn't rely on endless self-reflection? Externalization offers that possibility. By drawing their anxiety, naming it, and separating themselves from it, a person can begin to heal from their symptoms. With distance from their problem, they can see it from a new perspective, finding new solutions and easing their suffering. Externalization might be just the tool someone needs to break free from their anxiety and reclaim their life.

One of the primary benefits of externalization is emotional balance. When someone is struggling with internal problems, it can be overwhelming and stressful. By externalizing their thoughts and emotions, the person can feel a sense of relief and peace. This emotional balance can help the person be more objective and clear-headed in their problem-solving efforts.

Another benefit of externalization is that it can improve self-control when managing symptoms and problems. When a person internalizes their problems, they may feel like they do not have control over what's happening to them. By externalizing their problems, the person can take a step back and view the situation objectively. This can help them identify areas where they can take action and regain control.

Externalization also offers new resources for addressing problems. Problem-solving can be challenging, especially when someone feels stuck. Externalization can help individuals identify new tools and resources they may not have considered before. By expanding their perspective, the person can find new solutions to their problems.

Here's an example to illustrate the idea of externalization and problem-solving:

Consider that someone is struggling with a difficult project at work and feeling stuck. They've tried all their usual problem-solving methods, but nothing seems to be working, and they're feeling increasingly frustrated and overwhelmed. Through externalization, they might begin by asking themselves questions like: "What is it about this project that's making it so difficult?" "What are some of the specific obstacles I'm facing?" "What resources do I have available to me that could help me overcome these obstacles?"

As they answer these questions, they might begin to see the problem in a new light. They may realize, for example, that part of the reason they're struggling is because they're trying to do too much on their own and could benefit from collaborating with others. Or they may discover a new tool or resource that they hadn't considered before, such as a software program that could help them streamline their work.

By externalizing the problem and looking at it from a fresh perspective, they can begin to identify new solutions and resources that they may not have thought of before. This can help them feel more empowered and confident in their ability to solve the problem, reducing their feelings of frustration and overwhelm.

Taking responsibility for problems is another benefit of externalization. When someone feels overwhelmed by their difficulties, they may lose control of the situation. Externalization allows individuals to take responsibility for what they can change. By identifying their problems, externalizing them, and then taking action, the person can regain control of their life.

Externalization also allows people to question their beliefs and create new ways of thinking. Preconceived ideas can hinder progress, but by externalizing their problems, individuals can explore new ways of thinking and challenge their beliefs. By externalizing their thoughts and emotions, people can disassociate from the identity they gave themselves. For example, instead of thinking, "I'm always angry," they can think, "I get angry sometimes, but not always." This change in perspective can help them break free from negative self-talk and cultivate a more positive self-image.

Anxiety can be overwhelming and debilitating, leaving sufferers feeling helpless and hopeless. However, there is a technique that can help: narrative therapy. By externalizing one's anxiety and treating it like a separate entity, people can regain control and reduce its power over themselves. This type of therapy encourages individuals to tell their story from a different perspective, allowing them to gain insight into their feelings and behaviors. Rather than feeling trapped by their anxiety, those who practice narrative therapy can learn to reframe their experiences and see them in a new light. With patience and dedication, anxiety can be tamed, and a sense of calm and peace can be restored.

These four steps are part of the process of externalizing anxiety through narrative therapy.

The individual needs to begin by viewing their anxiety as an external force: The idea behind this step is to stop identifying with anxiety as if it is an integral part of one's personality or identity. Instead, they can treat it like an unwelcome visitor that comes and goes. This can help them to be less attached to it and to not take it personally. For example, instead of saying "I am an anxious person," one could say, "Anxiety is a feeling that comes and goes."

The second step involves naming one's anxiety: Naming anxiety can help people separate it from their sense of self and create some distance from it. It can also make it easier to identify when it shows up and how it affects them. For example, a person might call their anxiety "the worry monster." Now that the monster has been identified, **it's time to acknowledge how it affects them**. By acknowledging how anxiety affects them, they can gain more awareness of its impact on their thoughts, emotions, and behaviors. This can help them see how it is influencing their life and give them a starting point for making changes. For example, they could say, "When the worry monster shows up, I find it hard to concentrate on anything else, and it makes me feel tense and irritable."

So far, the worry monster has been identified and acknowledged. Now what? **Now it's time to prepare for a battle.** Start by *imagining yourself in a battle:* This step involves thinking about the strategies individuals have used in the past to combat anxiety, and coming up with new tools to try. By thinking of anxiety as an enemy to be fought, people can feel more empowered to take action against it. For example, one could say, "When the worry monster shows up, I use deep-breathing exercises and mindfulness to calm myself down. I also remind myself that worry won't change the outcome and try to focus on positive outcomes."

By externalizing anxiety through these four steps, people can change the way they think about it and take control of it. With practice, they can learn to respond to anxiety in more effective and healthy ways that allow them to live a more fulfilling life. Consider the below example:

Joan is a college student who struggles with test anxiety. Whenever she has a big exam coming up, she feels anxious and stressed out. Using narrative therapy, Joan takes the following steps:

- **Externalize her anxiety:** Instead of saying "I'm an anxious person," Joan thinks of anxiety as an external force that is bothering her. She tells herself, "Anxiety is making me feel nervous about this test."
- **Name her anxiety:** Joan decides to call her anxiety "the jitters." This helps her remember that it's something that comes and goes,

rather than a permanent part of her identity.

- **Acknowledge how it affects her:** Joan identifies how the jitters affect her thoughts, feelings, and behavior. She says, "The jitters make it hard for me to focus on studying. I feel jittery and restless, and I can't stop worrying about the test."

- **Imagine herself in a battle:** Joan thinks of herself as a warrior who is fighting against the jitters. She reminds herself of the strategies she has used in the past, such as taking deep breaths and visualizing success. She also thinks of new tools she can try, such as listening to calming music or going for a walk before the test.

By externalizing her anxiety, naming it, acknowledging how it affects her, and imagining herself in a battle against it, Joan is able to take control of her test anxiety, understand it, let it go and feel more confident and prepared for her exams. Over time, with practice, she is able to change her story about her anxiety and think and feel differently about it.

Chapter Takeaways

- People often find themselves engaging in a negative inner dialogue that seems to be on repeat. That's what Albert Ellis, the founder of rational-emotive-behavioral therapy, referred to as "stinking thinking." Negative scripts are essentially the pessimistic ways people think about themselves, others, or the world in general.

- Repetitive negative self-talk can trap individuals in past hurt and bitterness, as it strengthens pessimistic convictions about themselves and others. Persistently criticizing oneself and dwelling on unfavorable occurrences can establish a pattern of self-reproach and humiliation, which can generate a sense of powerlessness and despair.

- Externalization therapy is a type of therapy that assists individuals in separating themselves from the anxiety brought about by their distressing memories, enabling them to release their past experiences. In contrast to conventional therapies, externalization therapy promotes the idea of perceiving trauma as an external force, instead of an inherent aspect of oneself.

- One of the primary benefits of externalization is emotional balance. When someone is struggling with internal problems, it can be overwhelming and stressful. By externalizing their thoughts and emotions, the person can feel a sense of relief and peace.

Chapter 5: Moving Beyond the Hurt

In life, people are bound to encounter hurt and pain caused by others, and it can be challenging to move past these negative experiences. However, holding on to anger, resentment, and negative feelings can weigh people down and prevent them from living a fulfilling life. This chapter delves into the difficult yet freeing process of leaving toxic relationships behind and stepping into a brighter future. It is about learning to forgive those who have caused pain, and most importantly, about letting go of the resentment that holds one back. By gaining a new perspective, people can release themselves from the grip of bitterness and anger and move toward a place of healing and growth. It takes courage to break free from toxic people and the hurt they cause, but this chapter offers guidance and tools to help readers take that first step toward a healthier, happier life.

BREAK FREE FROM TOXIC PEOPLE

All individuals at some point in their lives have come across someone who left them feeling drained, frustrated, or even upset. These people are commonly referred to as "toxic." Recognizing and handling toxic people can greatly improve lives and pave the way for a healthier and more positive lifestyle. Unfortunately, dealing with toxic people is not always easy, as they can mask their behavior and intentions in ways that can be deceptive. But by identifying toxic traits and behaviors, people can better protect themselves and even reduce their own toxic tendencies.

Defining what it means to be a "toxic person" can be challenging because of the complexity of the traits and behaviors involved. A toxic person is skilled at deflecting responsibility and blaming others, preying on the goodwill or fear of others, and manipulating situations to their advantage. One common tactic of a toxic person is gaslighting, where they make someone else feel like they are the problem, causing confusion and self-doubt.

However, it is essential to recognize and define what constitutes toxic behavior to deal with negative relationships effectively. Labeling someone as a "toxic person" can be helpful in identifying harmful behavior patterns, but we must also be cautious not to attach judgment to an individual solely based on their actions. When dealing with toxic people, it is crucial to keep in mind that their behavior is not about *us*. Individuals should not tolerate toxic behavior, but they can respond in a way that respects both themselves and the other person's struggles. By setting boundaries and acknowledging the reasons behind someone's toxicity, people can maintain a healthy relationship or walk away from a harmful one with empathy and understanding.

Cutting out toxic people from one's life is an essential step toward maintaining one's well-being. Toxic individuals can cause mental and emotional exhaustion, chip away at one's self-esteem, and manipulate one's perception of reality. They can create a constant sense of stress and anxiety that can take a toll on an individual's mental and physical health. Studies have shown that people in negative relationships, including marital relationships, are at a greater risk of health problems such as heart disease. Stress and conflict can even impact your body's ability to heal wounds promptly (Kiecolt, 2005). With all these negative effects on the mind and body, it's clear that cutting toxic people out of one's life is crucial for maintaining positive relationships and overall good health.

Toxic people can have a contagious effect on those around them, even without realizing it. Whether it's a boss, friend, cousin, partner, or colleague, their negativity and manipulative behavior can slowly seep into one's own attitudes and actions. Has one ever found themselves feeling down after hanging out with someone who constantly complains? Or have they ever taken out their frustrations on a loved one after a tough day at work? These patterns are often unconscious, making them hard to recognize and even harder to break.

If one suspects that someone in their life may be toxic, they need to ask themselves the following questions: *Do I feel physically or emotionally exhausted after spending time with them? Am I uncomfortable at the thought of interacting with them? Do I feel less confident or satisfied with my life after interacting with them? Do they make me question me own beliefs and boundaries? Are my needs, thoughts, and feelings disregarded by them?*

Remaining in a toxic relationship can be incredibly damaging; therefore, it is very important to let go of these toxic people, as they may mimic the behaviors of abusers by offering temporary comfort, expressing remorse, and then repeating their harmful actions. This cycle can leave people with false hope, only to be repeatedly drawn back into the toxic relationship. Cutting off a toxic person can be a challenging decision to make, especially when there are many factors to consider. The setting and context of the relationship also play an important role in determining how to cut off a toxic person. For example, if someone works with a toxic colleague, cutting them off entirely may not be practical and could even harm their job performance. They may also have to tolerate a toxic cousin to maintain a relationship with the rest of their family.

However, people can still create boundaries to protect themselves from their negativity. They can set hard limits on the amount of time and energy they spend on the relationship, recategorize them in their mind, and draw clear boundaries around their interactions.

Ultimately, there is no perfect formula for cutting off a toxic person, but there are guiding principles to help people manage a difficult relationship. Individuals can start by determining the degree of distance they need from the person and then taking practical steps to protect themselves. It's important to prioritize one's physical and emotional well-being and seek support from people who uplift and empower them. Remember, cutting off a toxic person is an act of self-care and self-love, and everyone deserves to live a healthy, fulfilling life.

Determine the Degree of Distance

Determining the degree of distance is a crucial step in cutting off a toxic person from one's life. It's important to assess the relationship and understand the context and setting in which it exists. There are various degrees of distance that can be applied, depending on the situation and relationship.

One approach is to pull back on the amount of time one spends with the toxic person without formally notifying them of the decision. For instance, if someone has a toxic friend who constantly drains their energy and leaves them feeling emotionally drained, they could start by gradually reducing the amount of time they spend with them. This approach can help people create a functional relationship with the toxic person without exposing themselves to their negativity.

Another approach is to deal with the person at arm's length or through an intermediary. This is especially important in situations where the toxic person is a colleague or a dangerous partner in their personal life. For instance, if people have a toxic colleague, they could limit their interactions with them to the bare minimum required for their job.

Alternatively, one could delegate their interactions with them to another colleague where possible.

However, in some cases, the toxic person's behavior might be so egregious that the only way to protect oneself is to cease all contact with them. In such cases, one might need to formally distance themselves from them. This is particularly true in the case of toxic parents, longtime friends, or partners. This approach requires informing the toxic person that the relationship is changing and that their behavior needs to change if they want to maintain a relationship.

For example, if an individual has a toxic parent who has a history of emotional abuse and manipulation, they might need to tell them that they're taking a break from the relationship and that they need to respect their boundaries if they want to maintain a relationship with them. Similarly, if someone has a toxic partner who is physically or emotionally abusive, they might need to leave the relationship altogether to protect themselves.

In conclusion, determining the degree of distance is an essential step in cutting off a toxic person from one's life. It's important to assess the relationship and understand the context and setting in which it exists before deciding on the best approach. Cutting off a toxic person is never easy, but it's important to prioritize one's own well-being and mental health.

Draw a Boundary
Drawing boundaries is an essential step in cutting off a toxic person. It allows people to take control of the relationship and create a safe and healthy space for themselves. Here are some examples to help illustrate how to draw boundaries:

Let's say an individual has a friend who constantly belittles them and makes negative comments about their life choices. They might decide that they don't want to cut them out of their life completely, but they do need to set some boundaries around their interactions. They could tell their friend that they will no longer tolerate negative comments about themselves or their life, and that they need them to respect their choices. If they can't do that, the individual might have to limit the time they spend with them or avoid certain topics of conversation.

If someone has a toxic colleague who is always gossiping or spreading rumors, they might decide that they need to set some boundaries around their communication. They could tell their colleague that they're no longer interested in hearing or participating in gossip and that they will not engage in negative conversations about other coworkers. If they continue to behave inappropriately, they might limit their interactions with them to only work-related matters or seek the help of a supervisor or HR.

If one has a toxic family member who constantly invades one's personal space or disrespects their boundaries, they might decide that they need to create physical boundaries around their interactions. One could tell one's family member that they need them to respect their personal space and only visit or contact one when invited. One might also limit the amount of time they spend with them and make it clear what topics of conversation are off-limits.

In all these examples, the key is to identify what behavior an individual will no longer tolerate and communicate those boundaries clearly to the other person. It's important to stick to one's boundaries and enforce them consistently. This will help one create a healthy and safe space for oneself and send a message to the toxic person that their behavior is not acceptable.

Choose Your Method of Communication

Choosing the appropriate method of communication when cutting off a toxic person is crucial. The nature of the relationship and the potential risks involved will help determine the best medium for delivering the news. For example, if the toxic person is a partner, friend, or parent, an in-person conversation may be necessary. However, safety should always be a priority, and meeting in a public place could prevent the toxic person from becoming hostile or violent. It's also important to have witnesses around in case things turn for the worse.

On the other hand, if an individual is distancing themselves from a newer acquaintance or colleague, a brief email or text message may suffice. Written communication can also be helpful in documenting workplace conflicts or legal situations. Writing a letter can be cathartic and allow one to express their thoughts more clearly without getting drawn into an argument.

In some exceptional cases, delivering the news through an intermediary may be necessary—for instance, if an individual asks a friend to tell a dangerous partner that they're moving on or if their boss needs to tell a problematic employee to stay away from them. However, it's important to consider the risks involved in involving a third party.

Ultimately, the best method of communication is one that reflects the relationship a person had with the toxic person, allows them to express themselves most clearly and safely, and achieves their objective. This could be a brief phone call, a text message exchange over a few days, or a fifteen-minute conversation in a public place. All these options are legitimate forms of communication.

Don't Overly Justify Your Decision

When cutting someone off, remember that one doesn't owe the other person a detailed explanation of their reasons. Overexplaining oneself can sometimes make the situation worse, as toxic people may use this information against them or try to argue against their decision. Instead, it's best to be clear and concise about one's decision, without getting drawn into an argument.

For example, if an individual is breaking up with a toxic partner, they might simply say, "I've decided that it's best for us to go our separate ways." They don't necessarily need to go into detail about every problem in the relationship. Similarly, if one is distancing themselves from a friend or colleague, a simple "I don't think this relationship is healthy for me" might be enough. It's important to remember that people don't need to convince the other person of their decision or justify it to them. It's one's own decision to make, and one has the right to communicate it in a way that feels safe and respectful to them.

Overall, the key is to be clear, concise, and respectful in one's communication. People should avoid getting drawn into an argument or trying to justify their decision too much. If the other person tries to argue or negotiate, it's perfectly acceptable to set a boundary and explain that one is not interested in discussing it further. After setting a firm boundary, it's only natural to **expect a response.** When people set boundaries or cut someone off, it's important to be prepared for their response. Toxic people often react negatively to these kinds of decisions, and their response may be extreme. It's important to understand that their reaction is not a reflection of one's decision. Individuals have the right to redefine the relationship and to prioritize their own well-being.

In some cases, the toxic person may try to maintain the relationship by violating the new boundaries one has set. They may ignore one's requests for space or privacy, or they may try to manipulate or guilt-trip one into maintaining contact. It's important to stay firm and consistent in one's decision and to seek support from friends or family if necessary. It's also important to be prepared for any feelings that their response may trigger. An individual may feel guilty, ashamed, or afraid, but it's important to remember that these feelings are normal and to be expected. Setting boundaries and standing up for oneself can be a difficult and unfamiliar experience, but it's also a sign of growth and self-care.

Let's say an individual has a friend who is always negative and brings that person down with their constant complaining and criticizing. They've tried talking to them about it and setting boundaries, but nothing has changed. They decided that they need to cut this person out of their life for their own mental health.

When that individual breaks the news to their friend, they might say something like, "Hey, I just wanted to let you know that I've decided to distance myself from our friendship. I don't feel like the relationship is healthy for me right now, and I need to focus on my own well-being. I wish you all the best."

In response, the friend might get angry and defensive, saying things like, "How could you do this to me? You're abandoning me when I need you the most!" Or they might try to bargain with you, saying, "I'll change, I promise! Please don't leave me!"

In either case, it's important to remember that their reaction is not a reflection of the decision the individual made for their own peace of mind. The individual has the right to prioritize their own mental health and well-being. It might be hard to deal with their response, but it's important to stand firm in one's decision and not let them guilt or manipulate one into changing their mind.

Therefore, it becomes very important to hold **one's boundaries.** Holding boundaries is the crucial next step after drawing boundaries with a toxic person. Maintaining boundaries requires individuals to defend the line they have drawn and limit the amount of time they spend with the toxic person, keep certain topics or experiences off-limits, or have no contact at all. It requires conviction and patience on one's part and vigilance for any small inroads that subtly breach the line they've drawn.

In the digital age, people must also protect themselves online, blocking the toxic person on social media or filtering their messages, and have a plan for how to respond. Social media is not just a means of communication but also a part of the real world, so the more potential contact one has with a toxic person digitally, the greater the chances that they'll explore themselves to further abuse or inadvertently give them more data or ammunition.

Communicating one's stance is the best approach to holding a boundary. An individual can say, "I'm sorry, but this isn't a conversation I'm able to have with you right now" or "I understand you're upset, but I'm not interested in rehashing an old argument" or "This is the way our relationship has to be now." The individual is well within their right to firmly restate their boundaries and end the interaction. The toxic person may try to renegotiate the boundaries, but they should not agree to renegotiate with a problematic person, as it's a common toxic trap. Holding one's boundaries firmly and consistently is the key to preserving one's well-being and safety.

Let's say there's a friend who constantly talks about their problems without ever asking how *you are doing* or showing interest in *your* life. This has been going on for a while, and it's starting to take a toll on one's mental health. You decide to draw a boundary with that toxic friend and let them know that they need them to listen to one, too, and have a more balanced friendship.

Initially, the friend might be defensive or upset. They might say things like, "But I thought you enjoyed hearing about my problems" or "You're being selfish for wanting me to focus on you." This is where holding the boundary comes in—you need to restate their position and communicate their needs clearly. You might say something like, "I care about you and want to support you, but I also need our friendship to be a two-way street. I need you to listen to me, too, and show an interest in my life."

From there, it's important to maintain your boundaries. If the friend continues to monopolize conversations and not show interest in your life, you need to be prepared to restate their boundaries and even limit the amount of time spent with them if necessary. It might be difficult at first, but holding your boundaries is crucial for maintaining your mental health and wellbeing in relationships.

LEARN TO FORGIVE

Forgiveness—often heard frequently in self-help or wellness circles, but what does it really mean? A lot of people might think that it means letting go of the past and moving on, but believe it or not, there's so much science and psychology behind every word related to forgiveness. Before learning how to forgive, it's important to clarify what forgiveness is *not*. The person who forgives doesn't have to become best friends with someone who has wronged them, and it doesn't mean what happened was okay. In fact, forgiveness is all about acceptance— accepting what happened without dwelling on what could or should have happened instead. It's about choosing to love from a distance, or even *letting go altogether*. By tuning into the science of forgiveness, people can learn so much about how it can benefit their own lives in the present and for the future.

Forgiveness can be a tricky thing to conceptualize. It's easy to hold on to grudges and resentments toward those who have wronged another. But research has found that forgiveness can be incredibly beneficial for our mental and emotional well-being (Worthington et al., 2007). The three common components of forgiveness include gaining a more balanced view of the offender and the event, decreasing negative feelings toward the offender, and giving up the right to punish them further. It's important to note that forgiveness doesn't mean excusing the offender's behavior or minimizing the harm they caused. Rather, it's about releasing oneself from the burden of anger and hurt. Sure, some may see forgiveness as a sign of weakness, but it actually takes a lot of strength and courage to let go of the pain and move forward. So, let's reframe forgiveness as a powerful act of self-care rather than a sign of weakness.

Forgiveness can be a tough pill to swallow sometimes, but it's a necessary part of being human. Ponder this: Have you ever held on to a grudge for so long that it started to consume your thoughts? Yeah, all humans have been there. The thing is, forgiveness doesn't just benefit the person the individual wants to forgive—it also frees the individual from the weight of the anger and hurt they've been carrying. It's like releasing a heavy load they've been carrying on their back for years. By letting go of one's resentment and judgments, forgiveness teaches people to live in the present moment and move on from the past. It's a hard lesson to learn, but once people do, life becomes a lot lighter and more joyful.

Forgiveness is often overlooked as an essential component of any relationship. Everyone has their own way of looking at the world, and as such, misunderstandings can easily occur. These misunderstandings can lead to feelings of anger, resentment, and disconnection. However, by actively practicing forgiveness, people can close these gaps and bring themselves closer to their loved ones. Whether it's a romantic partner or a friend, showing forgiveness is a powerful way to demonstrate empathy and understanding. It's not always easy, but in the end, it's always worth it. So, if one wants to build stronger, healthier relationships, make sure forgiveness is a cornerstone of one's approach.

To be honest, it's not easy to forgive someone who has hurt one deeply, especially if there was betrayal involved. It's natural to feel shock and anger, and those feelings should not be ignored or dismissed. People must give themselves permission to feel those emotions and allow themselves to process what has happened. By exploring the situation and acknowledging the impact of the betrayal, people can start to understand the reasons and context behind it. This understanding can be the first steppingstone toward forgiveness.

Forgiveness is a powerful tool when it comes to one's overall well-being. Studies have shown that when individuals reported higher levels of forgiveness, they also reported better health habits and less depression, anxiety, and anger (Toussaint et al., 2015). This is not limited to personal relationships; even in betrayed couples, greater levels of forgiveness were associated with stronger relationships and positive parenting outcomes. Perhaps most surprising, however, is the impact on our physical health. Those who reported higher levels of forgiveness also had lower white blood cell counts and hematocrit levels (Toussaint, 2015). These results highlight the importance of forgiveness for one's own well-being. People shouldn't let feelings of anger and vengefulness consume them, deciding instead to take control and choose forgiveness.

The Four Ds of Forgiveness

Forgiveness is a complex process that requires both emotional and interpersonal efforts. The emotional transformation of forgiveness involves the difficult task of relinquishing negative emotions associated with a perceived wrongdoing. This can be a challenging and painful experience, but ultimately allows individuals to move forward and let go of any resentments they may hold. Interpersonally, forgiveness involves finding *empathy and compassion* for the wrongdoer, though this does not necessarily mean that it requires interacting with them. The process of forgiveness is unique to each person, and the four Ds of forgiveness can be helpful tools to navigate through it.

The four Ds of forgiveness provide a structured approach to the process of forgiving someone. Each step allows one to reflect on their feelings, consider their options, and ultimately make a decision that is right for them.

The first step is **deep-diving**, and it involves developing more insight into the offense and its present impacts. This step requires the individual to write about the wrong that they have suffered and explore how it has affected them emotionally, mentally, and physically. For instance, let's say that a person has been cheated on by their partner. In this case, the person may write about the betrayal they have experienced and how it has impacted their trust, their self-esteem, and their sense of security. They may also explore the anger, sadness, and other emotions that have arisen as a result of the betrayal.

The second step is **deciding,** which involves considering what forgiveness means to one and electing to forgive—or not. The individual may reflect on forgiveness as a concept and decide what it means to them personally. For instance, forgiveness may mean letting go of resentment and anger toward the wrongdoer and accepting that what happened cannot be changed. Alternatively, forgiveness may mean reconciling with the person who has wronged one and working toward rebuilding the relationship. After weighing the benefits and downsides of forgiving, the individual can make a decision that feels right for them.

The third step, **doing**, involves taking the transgressor's perspective in an attempt to understand their motives and reconcile with one's own feelings. This step requires one to step into the other person's shoes and try to understand their actions from their point of view. For instance, if one's partner cheated on them, they may try to understand why they did it. Was it because they were unhappy in the relationship, or because they had personal issues they were struggling with? By trying to understand the other person's perspective, individuals can begin to find a path toward reconciliation.

The fourth step, **deepening**, involves discovering meaning in the event and how much one has grown from it. This step allows people to reflect on the benefits of forgiveness and how it has impacted their life positively. For instance, by forgiving their partner for cheating, one may have learned to communicate more effectively, set boundaries, and trust their instincts. Forgiveness can also bring a sense of peace and closure, allowing them to move on from the past and focus on the present.

In conclusion, the four Ds of forgiveness provide a useful framework for anyone who is struggling to forgive someone who has wronged them. By following these steps, people can develop more insight into the situation, make an informed decision, try to understand the other person's perspective, and find meaning and growth in the experience. Here's an illustrative example:

Deep-diving: Jane was deeply hurt when her best friend, Sarah, betrayed her trust. Sarah had shared some private information with others that Jane had confided in her. Jane felt violated and betrayed. The event caused her to feel angry and disappointed in Sarah. She was hesitant to trust anyone again, and her relationships with others were impacted.

Deciding: Jane reflected on what forgiveness meant to her. She realized that forgiveness did not mean that Sarah's actions were okay or that she was excusing her behavior. It meant that she was choosing to let go of the anger and resentment that she was carrying toward Sarah. She weighed the benefits and downsides of forgiving Sarah. The benefits of forgiveness were that she could move on from the pain and start to rebuild trust with others. The downside was that she was afraid that Sarah would repeat her behavior and hurt her again.

Doing: Jane tried to understand why Sarah had betrayed her trust. She considered Sarah's perspective and how she might be feeling. She reached out to her and expressed how her actions had impacted her. She listened to her perspective and apologized for any role she may have played in their falling out. They both came to an understanding and worked toward reconciling their friendship.

Deepening: As a result of forgiving Sarah, Jane felt a sense of relief and closure. She no longer carried the weight of anger and resentment toward her. She also learned that it was possible to forgive and move on from betrayal. She felt more resilient and confident in her ability to trust others. She also learned the importance of communicating her needs and boundaries in relationships. Overall, the experience helped her grow as a person and improve her relationships with others.

The Four Rs of Self-forgiveness

Self-forgiveness is an act of kindness and acceptance toward oneself for the wrong actions or decisions one may have made in the past. It is an acknowledgement that one is not perfect and that one can make mistakes, and that is okay. Unlike forgiving others, self-forgiveness requires introspection and the willingness to truly examine one's own thoughts and behaviors.

It means taking accountability for one's actions, letting go of guilt, and choosing to move forward rather than dwell on the past. While forgiving others involves releasing resentment toward them, self-forgiveness is about releasing negative feelings toward oneself and choosing to practice self-compassion. It may not be easy, but self-forgiveness is an important step toward inner peace, growth, and living a fulfilling life.

Following are a set of steps that can help individuals move forward after making mistakes or experiencing failures. Let's take a closer look at each step with some illustrative examples.

Responsibility

The first step in self-forgiveness is taking responsibility for one's actions. It involves acknowledging that one made a mistake, and accepting that one is accountable for the consequences of one's actions. Taking responsibility means avoiding excuses or shifting blame to others, and recognizing that one had control over one's decisions.

For example, let's say that an individual missed an important deadline at work because they were procrastinating. Taking responsibility would involve acknowledging that one didn't manage their time well and accepting that they let down their team by missing the deadline. It might be difficult to admit fault, but it's an important step in the self-forgiveness process.

Remorse

The second step in self-forgiveness is feeling genuine remorse for one's actions. Remorse is more than just feeling bad about what one did; it involves a deep sense of regret and sadness for the harm one caused. Feeling remorse shows that one recognizes the impact of one's actions on others and oneself. Using the same example, after acknowledging one's responsibility, one might feel genuine remorse for letting the team down. The individual might feel guilty for the inconvenience they caused and recognize that their procrastination affected not just themselves but their colleagues as well.

Restoration

The third step in self-forgiveness is taking steps to restore what was damaged. Restoration involves making amends or taking actions to make things right. This might involve apologizing to those one has hurt, or finding ways to repair the harm caused. In the previous example, restoration could involve working with one's team to find a solution that meets the original deadline, or going above and beyond to ensure that future deadlines are met. It might also involve having an honest conversation with their boss or colleagues to express their remorse and commitment to doing better in the future.

Renewal

The final step in self-forgiveness is renewal. This involves moving forward with a renewed sense of purpose and commitment to doing better in the future. Renewal is about learning from one's mistakes and using them as an opportunity to grow and improve. For example, after taking responsibility, feeling remorse, and working on restoration, you might make a renewed commitment to manage your time more effectively in the future. You might set specific goals and develop strategies to avoid procrastination, and actively seek feedback from colleagues to ensure that you're meeting expectations.

Overall, the four Rs of self-forgiveness are a powerful tool for overcoming feelings of guilt and shame and moving forward and letting go after making mistakes or experiencing failures. By taking responsibility, feeling genuine remorse, working on restoration, and committing to renewal, people can learn from their mistakes and become better versions of themselves.

Learning How to Forgive Yourself

Remember, self-forgiveness is not about letting oneself off the hook, nor is it a sign of weakness. Forgiveness implies that one accepts the behavior, accepts what happened, and is willing to move on with their life without brooding on circumstances that cannot be altered. Understanding one's emotions is an essential aspect of self-forgiveness. By becoming aware of the emotions one is experiencing and labeling them, one can reduce the intensity of their feelings, particularly those associated with guilt and shame. For instance, suppose an individual is struggling to forgive themselves for hurting a loved one's feelings. In that case, they may feel intense guilt and shame, but by labeling these emotions and recognizing that they are normal and healthy, one can begin to regulate them better.

Accepting responsibility for one's actions is another critical step in the self-forgiveness process. This involves acknowledging one's mistakes, including the harm they caused and any justifications or rationalizations they may have made to excuse their actions.

Accepting responsibility allows them to avoid negative emotions such as regret and excessive guilt. Suppose an individual lied to a friend and caused them pain. In that case, they may feel guilty and want to rationalize their behavior by claiming it was for their benefit. However, accepting responsibility involves admitting that lying was wrong and hurtful to one's friend.

Treating oneself with kindness and compassion is vital when working toward self-forgiveness. This means acknowledging one's mistakes while still showing compassion toward oneself. For example, if someone made a mistake at work that resulted in a significant loss for the company, that person may feel like a failure. However, treating themselves with kindness and compassion involves recognizing that everyone makes mistakes, and that they can use this experience as an opportunity for growth and improvement.

Expressing remorse for one's mistakes is also an essential part of the self-forgiveness process. Feeling guilty or remorseful is a natural reaction to wrongdoing, and it can serve as motivation to change one's behavior. It is essential to distinguish between guilt and shame because shame can make one feel like a bad person, leading to negative emotions such as worthlessness, addiction, depression, and aggression. On the other hand, guilt acknowledges that one did something wrong but does not undermine their intrinsic value as a person.

Making amends and apologizing is crucial when seeking self-forgiveness. If one's actions have hurt someone, making it right with them can help one move past their guilt and start the healing process. For instance, if an individual lied to a friend, they might apologize to the friend and make an effort to rebuild their trust. Learning from the experience and trying to do better in the future is the final step in the self-forgiveness process. Once the individual has acknowledged their mistakes, expressed remorse, and made amends, they can use this experience as an opportunity for growth and improvement.

If one lied to their friend, they could reflect on what led them to lie and how they can communicate more honestly in the future. By doing so, they can become a better person and avoid making similar mistakes in the future. Here's an example that covers all the steps of self-forgiveness. Let's say an individual had a falling out with a close friend because they said something hurtful to them. At first, one tries to brush it off and pretend like it didn't happen, but one can't stop thinking about it and feeling guilty.

Step 1: Understand Their Emotions

One starts to recognize and label their emotions—feeling guilty, ashamed, and regretful.

Step 2: Accept Responsibility for Their Actions

The individual realizes that what they said was hurtful and that it is their responsibility to apologize and make things right.

Step 3: Treat Themselves With Kindness and Compassion

The individual tries to approach the situation with self-compassion, acknowledging that they made a mistake but also recognizing that everyone makes mistakes sometimes. One reminds themselves that they are still a good person who is capable of doing better in the future.

Step 4: Express Remorse for Their Mistakes

The individual reaches out to their friend and expresses their sincere remorse for what they said. They acknowledge the pain they caused and take responsibility for their actions.

Step 5: Make Amends and Apologize

The individual offers a genuine apology to their friend and tries to make things right. They ask what they can do to make up for their mistake and try to follow through on their suggestions.

Step 6: Learn From the Experience

The individual reflects on what happened and tries to understand why they said what they did. The friend in turn recognizes that the individual was feeling stressed and overwhelmed at the time, but that this was not an excuse for their hurtful words. The individual then brainstorms ways to manage their stress and emotions in the future so that they can avoid making similar mistakes.

Step 7: Try to Do Better

The individual commits to making an effort to do better in the future. They reflect on what they've learned and use this knowledge to guide their behavior going forward. They continue to check in with their friend and make sure that they are not repeating the same mistakes. By following these steps, the individual is able to take responsibility for their actions, show compassion to themselves, and work toward making things right with their friend. They also learned from their mistake and are committed to doing better in the future.

LETTING GO OF RESENTMENT THROUGH PERSPECTIVE-TAKING

Perspective-taking is the ability to step into someone else's shoes and view a situation from their point of view. This ability is a powerful tool for letting go of resentment, as it allows people to see the situation from a different perspective and understand where the other person is coming from. When people are caught up in their own feelings of hurt and anger, it can be difficult to see the other person's side of the story. However, by taking a step back and trying to understand their perspective, people can often find common ground and work toward forgiveness.

Perspective-taking is the ability to see things from another person's point of view. It is a crucial component of social interactions and communication and is essential for building relationships, empathy, and understanding (Galinsky, 2010). Shifting mental sets; as mentioned earlier, perspective-taking involves shifting from one's own mental state to that of another person. This ability to change mental sets is crucial for perspective-taking, and it requires executive functioning skills, such as working memory, attention, and cognitive flexibility.

For example, imagine a teacher who is frustrated with a student who is not paying attention in class. When the teacher tries to understand the situation from the student's perspective, however, they realize that the student might be going through a difficult time at home, and it is affecting their ability to focus in class. This shift in mental set allows the teacher to empathize with the student and address their needs more effectively.

Perspective-taking is a complex cognitive process that involves the activation of an entire network of brain regions. Research has shown that when people try to understand the mental states of others, the brain shows activation in several regions, including the dorsomedial and dorsolateral prefrontal cortices, temporoparietal junction, and precuneus (Wu et al., 2017).

For example, when a doctor is trying to understand a patient's symptoms, they might need to shift their mental set and consider the patient's medical history, lifestyle, and other factors that could be contributing to the symptoms. This requires the activation of several brain regions involved in social cognition, working memory, attention, and mental imagery.

Perspective-taking is essential for building empathy and understanding. When people try to see things from another person's point of view, they are more likely to empathize with them and understand their feelings and motivations. For example, when a couple is going through a difficult time in their relationship, they might need to practice perspective-taking to understand each other's needs and feelings. This could involve shifting mental sets, activating relevant brain regions, and building empathy and understanding for each other's perspectives.

In conclusion, perspective-taking is a crucial cognitive process that involves shifting mental sets, activating relevant brain regions, and building empathy and understanding for others. It is essential for social interactions and communication and can lead to better relationships, empathy, and understanding.

On the other hand, holding a grudge is dangerous but can be strangely satisfying. It allows people to feel superior, judging those who have wronged them and holding on to their resentment for weeks, months, or even years. According to C. Ward Struthers, a professor at York University who studies forgiveness, vengeance, and grudges, grudges are a form of self-protection. By holding on to negative feelings, people can use them to shield themselves from future harm.

Grudges are defined by Struthers as a sustained feeling of hurt and anger that can dissipate over time but can be reignited when needed. Robert Enright, a professor at the University of Wisconsin and a founding board member of the International Forgiveness Institute, explains that grudges exist on a spectrum. Some are easy to let go of, while others can grow into deep-seated hatred. Although Struthers believes that grudges can be held for a lifetime, Enright argues that forgiveness can release even the most profound resentments.

Understanding the process of how grudges are formed can be the first step in relinquishing their hold on one's life. Even if they're not ready to forgive, it's essential to recognize that grudges don't serve one's best interests and can have long-term negative consequences.

Elizabeth van Monsjou, a social psychologist who worked in Struthers's lab, identified common patterns among people who hold grudges. The journey toward harboring resentment begins with a *perceived wrongdoing or a harmful event*. The victim then feels inadequate and seeks validation by recounting the story to others. If the person is unable to let go and continues to ruminate on the event, a grudge can form. Negative thoughts and emotions about the wrongdoer and oneself begin to surface, and a breaking point ultimately leads to holding a grudge.

As time passes, the intense feelings of anger may dissipate, leading to the acceptance phase, where the person acknowledges holding a grudge. However, triggers such as a familiar song or memory can reignite the cycle of seeking validation and resentment. This cycle continues until the next trigger sets it off again.

To become nonchalant about wrongdoing and its perpetrator, it is necessary to have context and understanding of the situation.

Initially, after being hurt, one may feel raw and question why someone would mistreat them. Social psychologist Elizabeth van Monsjou advises attempting to understand the other person's motivation, which can be challenging. It involves considering what they thought of one's actions and how the wrongdoing affected their emotions. Van Monsjou cautions against judging the actions of others to reduce righteous indignation. It's less about judging the person and more about understanding what may have led to or contributed to the wrongdoing in that case.

Enright suggests that the transgressor may have unintentionally hurt another. By putting the event into perspective, one may realize that it was not as significant as they initially believed and they can now move on. He further postulates that the person who caused the harm may not have intended to do so. Perhaps their child was sick, and they forgot about the planned charity event, which was essential to them but not as crucial to them at the time. By putting oneself in their shoes, one may come to see that the event was not as significant as one initially believed and can move forward.

Perspective-taking is critical, as it adds shades of grey to black-and-white thinking that reinforces the idea that someone must be inherently bad if they have wronged one. If individuals only view things as good or bad, they won't be able to change their minds. However, if they remain open, flexible, and even curious, they can view things from many different points of view. However, seeing things from another person's perspective can be challenging, as individuals are often familiar with their thoughts and feelings, making it difficult to put them aside and understand someone else's point of view. To try to understand different perspectives, people can follow certain steps.

The first step in seeing things from different points of view is to identify the conflict that is happening. Start by thinking about the situation, who is involved, and how it makes one feel. This could be a conflict with a friend, family member, co-worker, or even a stranger. Write down all thoughts and feelings about the conflict, including any actions one may want to take. The goal here is to gain clarity about the situation, so be as honest as possible with oneself.

It's important to understand what's underlying the conflict one is experiencing. For instance, if an individual is upset because a friend canceled plans with them, it might not just be about the canceled plans. It could be that the individual is feeling neglected, unimportant, or even rejected. Understanding these deeper emotions can help people to approach the situation in a more constructive way.

Once the individual has gained some clarity about their own perspective, it's time to consider the other person's point of view. Try to put oneself in their shoes and imagine how they see the situation. Think about what their intentions may have been and how they may be feeling about the conflict. It can be helpful to write about this perspective as well, to really solidify it in one's mind. For example, if a coworker took credit for one's work, try to imagine why they may have done this. Perhaps they felt pressure to perform well or were worried about losing their job. Maybe they didn't realize the impact it would have on others. By understanding their perspective, one can begin to approach the situation in a more empathetic way.

After taking the time to consider the other person's perspective, return to one's own. Answer the questions from Step 1 again and see if one's answers have changed. *Did considering the other person's point of view help them see the conflict in a different light? Are there any steps they can take to resolve the situation that they didn't consider before?* It's possible that this exercise has helped one to gain a new perspective and approach the situation in a more constructive way.

By seeing things from different points of view, people can gain a deeper understanding of themselves and others. It can help them in approaching conflicts in a more constructive way and ultimately lead to more positive outcomes. Here's a more detailed example:

Step 1: Janet is having a conflict with her roommate, Sally. They have been arguing about the cleanliness of the apartment. She feels that Sally is not doing her fair share of the cleaning, and she is frustrated and angry. She wants to talk to her about the issue, but she's not sure how to approach it without causing an argument.

Janet takes a few minutes to write down her thoughts and emotions. She realizes that the underlying issue is not just about the cleaning but also about feeling disrespected and undervalued by Sally. Janet knows that she wants to find a way to communicate her feelings to Sally without making her defensive.

Step 2: Janet tries to put herself in Sally's shoes. She thinks about how Sally might see the conflict. Sally might feel that she is doing her part in cleaning, but maybe she has a different idea of what "clean" means. She might feel attacked by Janet's comments, and that could be why she's defensive. Janet thinks that Sally might be feeling overwhelmed by school and work, and she might not have enough energy to keep up with the cleaning. Janet takes a few minutes to write down her thoughts from Sally's perspective.

Step 3: After reflecting on Sally's perspective, Janet returns to her own. She realizes that she needs to approach the issue in a different way. Instead of accusing Sally of not doing her fair share, she needs to express her own feelings and needs in a calm and respectful manner. Janet decides to talk to Sally and start the conversation by acknowledging her own role in the conflict. She plans to tell Sally that she values their friendship and living arrangement, but she needs more help with the cleaning. She wants to listen to Sally's perspective and work together to find a solution that works for both of them.

In this example, Janet was able to use perspective-taking to understand the conflict from Sally's point of view, which helped her approach the issue in a different way. This led to a more productive conversation and a potential solution to the conflict.

Tips for Improving One's Ability to Jump into Another Person's Point of View

Tip 1: Watch a movie or TV show. Engaging with stories can be a great way to practice perspective-taking, and research has shown that reading and watching fiction are beneficial for developing empathy and perspective-taking. To start, choose a movie or TV show and select one of the character's perspectives to take. It can be helpful to start with a character who one feels is similar to oneself and then gradually try taking the perspective of characters who are very different from one.

As one watches the movie or TV show, pause it one third of the way through, half of the way through, and three fourths of the way through. Each time the individual pauses, they need to ask themselves what the character is thinking, why they are behaving the way they are, and what emotions they are experiencing. After one finishes watching the movie or show, assess how well one was able to identify with the character by asking oneself questions such as whether they were able to understand the events in the story in a manner similar to that in which the character understood them, whether they had a good understanding of the character, and whether they could feel the emotions the character portrayed.

Practicing perspective-taking with fictional characters can be easier than doing so with co-workers or people in one's own life because the narrative is designed to make one relate to and sympathize with some of the characters. Additionally, a person may not be as emotionally invested in the outcomes for fictional characters as in their own life. Once they become more comfortable taking on the perspectives of fictional characters and trying to understand their mental states, they can try using the same tactic in situations they encounter in their day-to-day interactions.

For example, if an individual has trouble understanding why a colleague is behaving a certain way, they can try to put themselves in their shoes and think about what might be going on in their life or what their thought process might be. This can help the individual better understand their perspective and improve their ability to see another person's point of view.

Good Will Hunting is a great movie to practice perspective-taking because it has complex characters with varying backgrounds and experiences. Consider this: An individual wants to practice perspective-taking with Will, the main character. He's a genius but also has a troubled past and struggles with intimacy and vulnerability.

As the individual watches the movie, they pause it at one third of the way through, half of the way through, and three fourths of the way through. Each time they pause it, they need to ask themselves:

- *What is Will thinking right now, and why?*
- *Is he feeling angry, sad, happy, or something else?*
- *What might be going on in his mind that led him to think or feel that way?*
- *Why is Will behaving the way he is behaving?*

- *Is he lashing out, being defensive, or pushing people away?*
- *What might be motivating his actions?*
- *What emotions is Will experiencing right now, and why?*
- *Is he scared, hurt, frustrated, or something else?*
- *What might be causing him to feel that way?*

Once the individual finishes the movie, they need to ask themselves these questions:

- *Was I able to understand the events in the movie in a manner similar to that in which Will understood them?*
- *Do I think I have a good understanding of Will's character?*
- *What motivates him, and what are his fears and insecurities?*
- *Did I tend to understand the reasons Will did what he did? For example, why he was reluctant to accept help from others, or why he was so defensive about his intelligence.*
- *Did I feel like I could really get inside Will's head and understand his perspective?*

- *Could I feel the emotions Will portrayed? For example, his anger or vulnerability in different situations.*
- *At key moments in the story, did I feel like I knew exactly what Will was going through?*

By practicing perspective-taking in this way, people can start to better understand the motivations and experiences of other people, even if they are very different from one's own. This can help them develop more empathy and be more effective in their real-life interactions with others.

Tip 2: Use Social Imagination

Using one's social imagination involves putting oneself in the shoes of others and trying to understand their thoughts, emotions, and behaviors in a given situation. This technique can help people see things from different perspectives and increase their ability to empathize with others.

One way to practice this is through a role-taking task, like the one described above. For example, let's say a person comes across a picture of a man holding a gun to another man's head, with two other men standing nearby. At first glance, one may assume that the man with the gun is a criminal and the other two men are innocent victims. However, using one's social imagination, they can try to see the situation from each character's perspective.

First, one can write down a dramatic story about what led up to the event and what is happening in the moment, including the outcome. Then, they can rewrite the story from the perspective of each character, starting with the man with the gun, then the man with the tie, and finally the man with his back to the camera. For each perspective, they should consider what the character is thinking and feeling, and how their unique inner narrative affects their actions and behaviors.

Once done, they read over the stories they wrote down and reflect on how well they were able to shift perspectives between the different characters. *Were they able to maintain continuity between the stories? Did they accurately describe the characters' mental states and motivations?* If an individual struggles with this exercise, they can try practicing with different images or scenarios to improve their social imagination skills.

By using their social imagination, one can improve their ability to see things from different perspectives and develop empathy for others. This can be particularly helpful in social situations where understanding another person's point of view is important for effective communication and building relationships.

Here's another example:

Imagine being a supervisor at a restaurant and one of the employees is constantly coming in late to work. Take a few minutes to imagine the situation from different perspectives:

From the employee's perspective: *What might be causing the employee to be consistently late to work? Is it due to personal issues, such as transportation or family obligations, or is it a lack of motivation to be punctual? How might the employee be feeling about their tardiness? Are they frustrated with themselves or embarrassed to be constantly late? What could you do as a supervisor to help address the situation while also being empathetic to the employee's situation?*

From the customer's perspective: *If the employee's tardiness is affecting the customer experience, how might they be feeling about the situation? Are they frustrated or annoyed at the slow service? Are they likely to return to the restaurant if the issue persists? What steps can you take to ensure the customer experience is not negatively impacted while also addressing the employee's behavior?*

From the business owner's perspective: *How might the employee's tardiness be affecting the business as a whole? Is it impacting productivity or the bottom line? What policies or procedures can be put in place to prevent future tardiness and ensure employees are held accountable?*

By considering the situation from multiple perspectives, people can gain a better understanding of the issue and potential solutions that can benefit all parties involved.

Tip 3: Practice perspective-taking in one's personal life

Tip 3 emphasizes the importance of practicing perspective-taking in one's daily life, particularly when dealing with conflicts. To better understand the other person's perspective, one can start by reflecting on the most recent conflict they had with someone or a current conflict they are experiencing.

First, take some time to write down what happened between the individual themselves and the other person. Then, try to identify what one did that might have caused the conflict. Put oneself in the other person's shoes and consider what they might have been thinking or feeling about one's actions. How might the conflict have affected their emotions?

Lastly, think about what one could have done differently from their perspective to avoid or resolve the conflict. By doing this exercise, one is able to set aside their own perspective and gain insight into how others perceive their behavior. Practicing perspective-taking in this way can help improve one's relationships and communication with others. It can also help reduce feelings of conflict and negativity. By understanding and empathizing with other people's perspectives, people can find common ground and work toward resolving issues together.

Consider that one recently had a disagreement with a co-worker. One can use this conflict as an opportunity to practice perspective-taking. First, they need to think about the conflict from the perspective of their co-worker. Write down the following:

What happened between you and your co-worker?
Example: You and your co-worker had a disagreement over how to approach a project.

What did you do to incite this conflict?
Example: You insisted on your approach and were dismissive of your co-worker's ideas.

What might your co-worker have been thinking about your actions?
Example: Your co-worker might have felt disrespected and undervalued and thought that you didn't value their input.

How do you think this conflict affected your co-worker's emotions?
Example: Your co-worker might have felt frustrated, angry, and discouraged.

From your co-worker's perspective, what could you have done differently during this conflict?
Example: You could have been more open to your co-worker's ideas and expressed appreciation for their input.

By thinking about the conflict from one's co-worker's perspective, one may be able to gain a better understanding of their feelings and motivations. This, in turn, can help one approach the conflict in a more constructive way and potentially resolve it in a way that benefits both parties. It's important to note that perspective-taking is not about assigning blame or absolving yourself of responsibility. Rather, it's about gaining a deeper understanding of a situation and approaching it with empathy and an openness to different perspectives.

Chapter Takeaways

- A toxic individual is an adept practitioner of dodging accountability, shifting blame onto others, exploiting others' good intentions or fears, and manipulating situations for their benefit. One of the typical methods employed by toxic people is gaslighting, whereby they lead others to believe that they are at fault, inducing bewilderment and self-questioning.
- Forgiveness does not entail the restoration of a close relationship with the wrongdoer, nor does it indicate that the offense committed was permissible. Instead, forgiveness involves acknowledging the reality of what transpired and refraining from dwelling on alternate scenarios. It entails opting to love from afar or, in some instances, even letting go completely.
- Perspective-taking is the ability to see things from another person's point of

view. It is a crucial component of social interactions and communication and is essential for building relationships, empathy, and understanding.

- Toxic individuals can cause mental and emotional exhaustion, chip away at one's self-esteem, and manipulate one's perception of reality. They can create a constant sense of stress and anxiety that can take a toll on an individual's mental and physical health.

Summary Guide

<u>CHAPTER 1: THE ART OF LETTING GO</u>

- Letting go is often used in psychology to describe the process of releasing attachment to something or someone. It may refer to letting go of negative thoughts, emotions, or behaviors that hold an individual back from reaching their full potential.
- The dichotomy of control is a central concept in Stoic philosophy that emphasizes the importance of distinguishing between things that are within one's control and things that are beyond one's control.
- One essential component of the Stoic philosophy's dichotomy of control involves developing an unwavering concentration on the present moment. This involves instructing one's mind to remain wholly involved in the current experience, rather than being sidetracked by concerns or

remorse about the past, or concerns or anticipation for the future.

- Nonjudgmental thinking is the practice of acknowledging and identifying one's thoughts without affixing any characterizations or viewpoints to them. This mindset is crucial when it comes to letting go, as it empowers individuals to look at their experiences objectively and without any partiality.

- Psychological distancing, also called self-distancing, pertains to the capability of creating distance between oneself and the cause of intense emotions or conflict. This involves adopting a more impartial outlook on a circumstance and thinking about one's choices instead of being swiftly swayed by emotions or urges.

CHAPTER 2: BREAKING THE CHAINS OF NEGATIVITY

- The notion of the inner critic is a well-known concept in psychology that pertains to the pessimistic voice that often exists within our minds. This voice evaluates, disapproves, and rebukes us for our perceived deficiencies and limitations.

- Patrick Gaudreau, a psychology professor at the University of Ottawa, introduced the concept of excellentism. It entails establishing lofty benchmarks for oneself, but not letting those standards become unrealistic or harmful to one's health. Instead of self-criticism when falling short, individuals can opt to embrace novel experiences, utilize innovative approaches to problem-solving, and learn from their errors as they persistently aim for excellence.
- Nonattachment is a technique of relinquishing the urge to manage, cling to, or possess things in life. It does not imply becoming disconnected or apathetic, but rather accepting that everything in life is transient and in a constant state of flux. By releasing attachment, individuals can encounter greater independence and less distress.

- The expression conscious media consumption pertains to the practice of being attentive and purposeful about the media that individuals choose to consume and how they consume it. Stephanie Harrison suggests that this requires individuals to pay attention to both the content of what they consume and their manner of consumption.

CHAPTER 3: THE GROWTH MINDSET

- The adoption of change is vital to a growth mindset because it enables individuals to consider challenges and setbacks as occasions for learning and advancement. A growth mindset is a conviction that one's skills and intellect can be enhanced through persistent effort, devotion, and determination. People who embrace a growth mindset regard failure as a momentary obstacle and utilize it as a platform for progress and advancement.

- Altering one's perspective on failure to perceive it as a learning prospect is essential to releasing apprehension regarding change. By regarding failure as an invaluable occurrence, individuals can assimilate lessons from their errors and modify their approach to boost their prospects of success in the future. This helps them steer clear of reiterating the same mistakes or getting trapped in similar circumstances.
- Brain dumping, a tool popularized by David Allen, is a technique to help organize one's thoughts and close any lingering "open loops" in one's mind.
- Brain dumps allow people to clear their mind of unnecessary worries and tasks. When someone has a lot on their plate, everything can feel urgent and important, which can leave them feeling overwhelmed and stressed. By taking the time to write down everything that's on one's mind, they'll gain a better perspective on what's truly important and what can wait.

- People often find themselves engaging in a negative inner dialogue that seems to be on repeat. That's what Albert Ellis, the founder of rational-emotive-behavioral therapy, referred to as "stinking thinking." Negative scripts are essentially the pessimistic ways people think about themselves, others, or the world in general.
- Repetitive negative self-talk can trap individuals in past hurt and bitterness, as it strengthens pessimistic convictions about themselves and others. Persistently criticizing oneself and dwelling on unfavorable occurrences can establish a pattern of self-reproach and humiliation, which can generate a sense of powerlessness and despair.
- Externalization therapy is a type of therapy that assists individuals in separating themselves from the anxiety brought about by their distressing memories, enabling them to release their past experiences. In

contrast to conventional therapies, externalization therapy promotes the idea of perceiving trauma as an external force, instead of an inherent aspect of oneself.

- One of the primary benefits of externalization is emotional balance. When someone is struggling with internal problems, it can be overwhelming and stressful. By externalizing their thoughts and emotions, the person can feel a sense of relief and peace.

CHAPTER 5: MOVING BEYOND THE HURT

- A toxic individual is an adept practitioner of dodging accountability, shifting blame onto others, exploiting others' good intentions or fears, and manipulating situations for their benefit. One of the typical methods employed by toxic people is gaslighting, whereby they lead others to believe that they are at fault, inducing bewilderment and self-questioning.

- Forgiveness does not entail the restoration of a close relationship with the wrongdoer, nor does it indicate that the offense committed was permissible. Instead, forgiveness involves acknowledging the reality of what transpired and refraining from dwelling on alternate scenarios. It entails opting to love from afar or, in some instances, even letting go completely.

- Perspective-taking is the ability to see things from another person's point of view. It is a crucial component of social interactions and communication and is essential for building relationships, empathy, and understanding.

- Toxic individuals can cause mental and emotional exhaustion, chip away at one's self-esteem, and manipulate one's perception of reality. They can create a constant sense of stress and anxiety that can take a toll on an individual's mental and physical health.